An Unsettled Country

An
Unsettled
Country

Changing Landscapes
of the
American West

Donald Worster

A Volume in the Calvin P. Horn Lectures
in Western History and Culture

University of New Mexico Press / *Albuquerque*

Library of Congress Cataloging-in-Publication Data

Worster, Donald, 1941–
    An unsettled country : changing landscapes of the American West /
Donald Worster. — 1st ed.
        p.   cm. — (Calvin P. Horn lectures in western history and
culture)
    Includes bibliographical references and index.
    ISBN 0-8263-1481-3. — ISBN 0-8263-1482-1 (pbk.)
    1. Landscape—West (U.S.)—History. 2. Man—Influence of
environment—West (U.S.)—History. 3. Man—Influence on nature—
West (U.S.)—History. 4. West (U.S.)—History. 5. West (U.S.)—
Geography. I. Title. II. Series.
F591.W876   1994
978—dc20   93-30331
                                                           CIP

For Wallace Stegner (1909–1993)

Contents

Preface

The American West gets complicated if we think about it. The West, we like to say, is a place unlike any other—more colorful, more heroic, more immense in vistas. Yet it is also a cluster of places that can be radically different from each other, as different as the Staked Plains of Texas are from the Upper Yellowstone river valley; and it is a place offering many ecological similarities to regions on many continents, from Africa to Australia. The West, we also boast, is a place we humans have created out of raw matter with our minds and labor. In fact it is more than our creation: it is the work of nature, too.

None of the West's major landforms—from the loess beds of Nebraska, to the Grand Canyon, to the California coastal plate pushing north toward Alaska—is the product of human effort. We could never have made any of them. Consider the amount of labor it would take merely to move Point Reyes to Mendocino and one sees the limited role people can play in making the place. We have named the region the "American West"—using English and Italian words, and we have carved out cities and states that bear other names. The work we have done in settling the region has changed the chemistry of the soil and air, as they have the populations of fauna and flora, and these are not negligible achievements. But such cultural creations form only part of the landscape, and undoubtedly in the long run they are not even the most enduring part.

Much of what we mean by the West is what we have found there in a state of nature. The quality of light and shadows falling over the land inevitably comes to mind when we think of the region. Or the way bunchgrasses and sagebrush disperse across the dry earth, forming patterns based on millions of years of biological evolution. Or the West is the sound of mountain water to our ears, the smell of dust in our nostrils, the sight of vast lava beds stretching to the horizon. All of those elements of nature become sensations in the human mind and stimulate wonderfully rich ideas and feelings; but to restrict the place only to those inner meanings would be extremely arbitrary. A place like the West must be discovered as well as invented.

Our culture, both in its popular and elite forms, frequently denies this more complex truth. For example, one of John Ford's film masterpieces, *The Man Who Shot Liberty Valance*, released in 1962, illustrates how popular storytellers have sometimes forgotten what truly has made the West what it is. The story opens on a scene of bustling civilization, filled with railroads, brick buildings, and middle-class homes that have replaced the wild frontier. Most of the rest of the movie is a flashback to explain how it all happened. Violent men once fought for supremacy, the film recalls, but law won out. The town moved from rule by might to rule by democratic elections. According to the film, the story of the West is one of turning nature into artifact. As the leading female character says near the end, looking from a railroad car window onto the improved scene, "It was once a wilderness, now it's a garden."

By modern ideas of justice, Ford may not seem adequately enlightened because he puts white males in the foreground of that creative process. Today, many historians would insist that the making of the West must be seen as the work equally of women and of men, and of Indians, Hispanos, African-Americans, and other citizens, too. But commonly historians along with filmmakers, liberals along with conservatives, and humans of all varieties agree on one conclusion: nature was passive and ineffectual, a blank slate without form or meaning, before humans arrived, and the land contributed nothing to the triumph of civilization. Human imagination and human labor have made the region what it is and have given meaning to the West.

The essays in this book are arguments against that view of the West as a simple cultural invention. They try to demonstrate, in a series of case studies, how the natural environment has played an active, crucial role in the making of the West—and often in its unmaking and remaking. They are not arguments for the counter-simplification of environmental determinism, which maintains that nature has been all-powerful in shaping human life. I acknowledge that the region is inconceivable without its people, that those people have helped bring it into being, that the West is the product of political, economic, and cultural negotiation among many groups, that the West today is to a large extent a cultural achievement. I do not believe, however, that the West is simply "the work" of those groups. From its earliest settlement by ancient peoples from Asia to its latest immigrants it has always involved a dialogue with nature, a process of discovery and adaptation.

The first chapter pursues that argument through an analysis of the ideas of John Wesley Powell, whose chief contribution was to discover the powerful fact of aridity in the region and to reflect on its implications for the region's future. Powell's opponents were radical "constructionists"; that is, they were politicians, businessmen, miners, and farmers intent on constructing a region to fit their dreams, a construction that would be limited only by the availability of capital and technology. Powell came to a different conclusion, one emphasizing the need for adaptation to the land similar to what bioregionalists call for today, where region is the outcome of a dialogue between culture and nature. In the second chapter I examine the whites' drive to control the region's scarce water supply, a drive rooted in western European imperial thinking and carried by imperialists to many parts of the globe, always with the same extravagant ambitions and the same disappointing results. However, if people could not quite construct the endlessly green land they sought in the desert, they could and did have a devastating effect on the wild animals. In another chapter I describe that devastation that took place in the last century. Even there, contrary to the settlers' expectations, the animals did not simply go extinct; most species survived the ferocious assault of gun and plow, many have even rebounded in numbers, and with the help of conservationists they are still in the West, struggling to live with us today. In the last chapter I look at that vast subregion called the Great Plains, where human labor has been so vigorously expended to create something agricultural, something productive, out of what was once dismissed as a dreary wasteland. Droughts have repeatedly interfered with that work, however, spoiling it and setting it back; and today, complicating the already complex natural patterns of rainfall and aridity, patterns that we have hardly begun to understand, humans may be inadvertently causing a process of global warming, with immense implications for western life.

The conclusion from these studies is that the West remains a highly unstable place, changing constantly, reacting to the forces of nature as much as culture, never arriving at a point of being "settled." The work of creating any region is one of mind and matter interacting with each other. The result can be quickly undone by the processes of nature, or by our own folly, or by new technological breakthroughs. A history of the West that does not start from that dialectical perspective, I believe, is both naive, simplistic, and arrogant.

Portions of these chapters were delivered as the Calvin P. Horn Lectures in Western History and Culture of 1992 at the University of New Mexico. I want to thank the audience attending those lectures for offering many useful comments and the director of the Center for the American West, Richard Etulain, for his thoughtful and generous hospitality during my stay. He and his colleagues in the History Department at New Mexico have created one of the country's most important, lively programs for the study of the West. The staff at the University of New Mexico Press has been an impressive group to work with, including Beth Hadas, David Holtby, Larry Ball, and Emmy Ezzell. I also owe a large debt to my capable research assistants, James Pritchard and Paul Witzel of the University of Kansas.

Finally, a painful note about the dedication: as I was completing the revisions of this book, news came that Wallace Stegner had died in a Santa Fe hospital following an automobile accident. For me he was the most significant writer about the American West in this century, a visionary of tempered hope, a novelist and historian of eloquence and insight, a conservationist whose moral leadership deeply touched me as it did many others. "While the West is admitting its inadequacy," he once wrote, "let it remember its strength: it is the New World's last chance to be something better, the only American society still malleable enough to be formed." I do not know whether I can share all that is implied in those words, but I do know how much I respected, and needed, the man who wrote them. Whatever can be said about the region, this man who loved it had no serious inadequacy. Let us long remember his remarkable gifts, his love of the place, and his critical voice about its future.

D.W.
Rock Creek, Kansas
April 1993

1

The Legacy of
John Wesley Powell

Westward-moving pioneers, creaking in covered wagons along the Oregon and Santa Fe trails of the last century, came into a country of raw physical nature, less mediated by the forces of life than that on the eastern side of the continent. The sheltering forests thinned out, then disappeared over most of the terrain, leaving the earth exposed like a massive brown body, every crevice, bulge, and scar from the past relentlessly revealed. Many travelers felt themselves exposed, like Adam and Eve, but without any fig leaves growing in the neighborhood. Even the grass seemed too short and sparse to shelter them from cosmic eyes.

As farmers they had seen cleared-off lands before and were familiar with the earth's anatomy, but beyond the Missouri River the landscape was shockingly bare. It was not a cleared space at all, shaped and controlled by human labor and softened by human habitation, or even by vegetation, but a landscape vividly expressing its unrestrained power: an overwhelming sky, swift-moving clouds, wide-swinging rivers, rugged buttes and mountains, vast desiccated plains, all expressing a geophysical power that completely dominated the vulnerable numbers of plants and animals. The pioneers encountered some of the world's driest deserts, victimized by unrelenting atmospheric currents that pulled water vapor from the distant Pacific Ocean, dropped it in the high Sierras and Rockies, and left the low-lying lands parched and deadly. This elemental landscape presented an altogether new kind of wildness beyond European or eastern American experience, which had long been defined as a struggle to create farms out of dark green forests. The West was a more extreme wildness—sunlight against shadow, heat against cold, granite against water.

The western lands were not only big, brown, bare, and imposing; they also confronted the traveler with a time scale that was older than anyone had once supposed possible. The earth's many species, scientists had begun to realize by the early nineteenth century, had existed long before the year 4004 B.C., which was Archbishop James Ussher's calculation for the year of creation; bones dug from the ground proved how wrong he was. But the earth itself was far, far older than any kind of animal fossil. Scientists had begun talking about an ancient Devonian time, a Cambrian period of history, a Precambrian period, and closer to the present, a Carboniferous, a Triassic, a Jurassic, a Cretaceous period. Life had appeared only in the later phases of that history.

This was a revolutionary chronology. Western travelers familiar with some of its implications, and surely there were a few such among the hundreds of thousands that went west, had to realize that this new country was not new at all. They were traveling back in time as well as forward to opportunity. From a wagon seat a pioneer looked out on loessial plains of dust blown in at the end of last Ice Age. She peered into canyons cut through layers of rock deposited back in those unimaginable eras of the past; faced mountains uplifted by tectonic powers that we have begun to understand only in the last few decades; passed over hidden seas and rivers buried hundreds of feet underground, their signature written in gravel and limestone beds that only modern deep-drilling rigs can actually touch, that no human will ever see. Today we have identified dates for the history of those landscapes, running back millions of years into the past, but no early pioneer, however educated, could have grasped just how immensely old the western land really was. A few, nonetheless, must have sensed now and then that they had entered a place where time had extended long before any civilization anywhere had appeared. The age of the great trek westward was also an age beginning to discover deep time, on a scientific and on a popular level, time beyond the mythology of Genesis. It was an age preparing to displace humans from the center of creation.

Among the many Americans who looked with intense interest and expectation toward the opening of this West was John Wesley Powell of Bloomington, Illinois. He had been born in 1834 in Mount Morris, New York, to English immigrant parents, and raised on a succession of farms in Ohio, Wisconsin, and Illinois. Early on he rejected the model of his father's career of Methodist evangelist, perhaps because he resented the hard farm labor he had to do when his father was away preaching, and had made himself, with little formal training, into a free-thinking scientist, a field geologist.[1] He read about the western lands from that rambling military man, John Charles Frémont, author (with his wife Jessie's help) of the *Report of the Exploring Expedition to the Rocky Mountains in the Year 1842*. The young Powell must have read this description of the Green River valley in what is now Wyoming:

> In the river hills of this place, I discovered strata of fossiliferous rock, having an *oolitic structure*, which, in connexion with the neighboring strata, authorize us to believe that here, on the west side of the Rocky mountains, we find repeated the modern formations of Great Britain and Europe, which have hitherto been wanting to complete the system of North American geology.[2]

Typical Frémontian description—vaguely authoritative, hurried and incomplete, pressing on to new adventures. It would have been enough, however, to stoke Powell's imagination with visions of himself on his knees in that same place, digging up and classifying those fossils, breathing the ambient mountain air, filling in the continent's geological system. Eventually he met and talked with Frémont and corresponded with scientists about western natural history. Increasingly bored with his life as a classroom teacher (teaching botany, comparative anatomy, systematic zoology, geology, and mineralogy) at Illinois Wesleyan University and then at Illinois State Normal University, Powell itched to be out among those magnificent rocks.

In the summer of 1867, Wes Powell was at last on his way west, guiding a group of undergraduate students and small-town amateur naturalists over the rutted plains along the Platte River, the route of the pioneers. They passed wagon trains filled with rural folk heading for productive homesteads. Powell, however, was aiming in a different direction—for the Badlands of Dakota, where the White River had cut deeply into fine, white, clay sediments intermixed with thin sandstone layers, a place no farmer could love. Powell must have seen in such a sterile but strangely beautiful place the possibilities of a good crop of scientific discovery. But at Fort Laramie, discouraged by reports of growing Indian resistance to white travelers, the party changed their minds and turned south into Colorado, looking for Pike's Peak. It was a momentous adjustment of course, for during that summer in the Colorado high country, Powell first heard about the unexplored reaches of the Colorado River, where erosion had worked on the grandest scale anywhere, where the river was reputed to disappear into vast subterranean conduits, where waterfalls larger than any ever seen by humans might thunder. What had begun as a college outing abruptly led to a new ambition to explore that fabled river through its canyons, whatever the risk, and add dramatic new knowledge to the American mind.

During the winter of 1867–68, Powell prepared for that next, bigger expedition. In late May 1869, at one o'clock in the afternoon, on the Green River not far from where Frémont had found those fossiliferous rocks, Powell and nine other men set off downstream on the mission that would make his name great. Had the Sioux been a little less resistant to interlopers, he might have been digging away in the Badlands or clambering around the Black Hills before George Armstrong Custer got there and discovered gold. Instead by the workings of circumstance and ambition, he became, with a remnant five of his men loaded into two little boats, the first American to navigate successfully the shadowed, dangerous labyrinth of the Colorado canyonlands. They came out of the labyrinth on August 30 at Grand Wash Cliffs, and Powell returned to the settlements a national hero.

In that decade of the 1860s, the American West began to emerge for the first time as a distinctive region of the country. For a long while it had been as mysteriously located as heaven or hell. West referred to a compass direction, a general trend of movement, a fantasy land rather than to any particular place with a particular past. As a study in popular mythology, that older, vaguer West was highly interesting, but it lacked concreteness and defied knowledge. After the Civil War, however, the vagueness began to disappear, and for the first time the West took shape as a distinctive new region of the United States.

The nation had had some prior experience with regionalism, though little of it good. During Powell's growing-up years, many local attachments, dating from colonial days, had been replaced by a rising nationalism, yet in those same years a common national identity had increasingly been thwarted by the growing confrontation of North against South. In the North people had become Yankees all, from Lawrence, Massachusetts, to Lawrence, Kansas, while in the slave-owning and trading South they had developed a strong sense of being different. We may call that complex process of fusion and fission by the name of sectionalism, which was the nineteenth-century term for any departures from a single national identity, or we may call it regionalism, a twentieth-century term; but the process was one and the same. By 1861 Americans had created two major ways of being American, based on disparities of environment, labor, race, and tradition, but then found they could not tolerate those differences. They fell into a war when the North tried to impose its definition of Americanness on the South, a war that left both regions bloodied and exhausted. Together they had made a botch of the Founding Fathers' dreams of a new unified civilization.

Had the re-United States in 1865 been forced to live within the confines of their old territory, they might still be nursing old grudges, always ready to divide and fight again, like the Czechs and Slovaks, the Serbs and Croats. But fortunately that was not to be; they had a vast expanse of land stretching westward from the Great Plains to the Pacific Coast that diverted their attention. All of that land was under American ownership. What could be made of it? How might it heal a wounded civilization? They called that great space "the West," meaning the part of the country where the passions of the Civil War had been less bitterly felt, the battlefields had been fewer, the old rivalries less rooted and intense. The West was wherever the North and South faded away. Its borders were still a little vague, of course, as regions always are, and the indefiniteness would persist for a long while, as settlers brought into the West their old identities, their bitterness, their tattered uniforms and wartime weapons. All the same they came in a spirit of forgetting the colossal failure of the war. The West would be neither North nor South, but a new, third way of being American. Simultaneously it would offer the promise of a new national unity, a new geography of hope, and a fresh beginning for a bankrupt nation.

Wes Powell was painfully aware of what the country had just been through. He had grown up in an abolitionist family and enlisted to fight as a private in the Illinois volunteer infantry before the war really began. On induction he was described as "age 27, height 5'-6-1/2 inches tall, light complected, gray eyes, auburn hair, occupation—teacher." A year later he was a company officer at the battle of Shiloh, Tennessee, when a minié ball struck him on the right arm, breaking the bones and embedding itself in the flesh so deeply it could not be removed. A druggist-become-war-surgeon amputated his arm just above the elbow. For the rest of his life, Powell would suffer frequent, intense pain in that stump of an arm, reminding him again and again of those fierce battle-fields, the heavy smell of gunsmoke, the groans of other wounded men lying in hospital beds. Maimed though he was, he had resolutely gone back to the war, leaving the army only in 1865, with the rank of major. Four years later he went down the Colorado River, the stump still throbbing, the trauma of sectional conflict a long way off but never to be forgotten. With others of his generation, he would seek a West beyond fratricide, at once familiarly nationalistic in its ambitions, yet a distinctly better regionalism than all that gone before.

Today John Wesley Powell's name is widely connected with the West, but what was his true significance for its development? In much of the popular literature, he appears as a romantic adventurer, little different from Frémont or Kit Carson. He was the last in a line of hero-explorers, we are told, who revealed the way west and opened up the country for American expansion; an agent of imperialism who helped "win" the West, handing it over to a grateful nation, then abruptly disappearing.[3] Other interpretations of Powell bring him into the twentieth century, but what did he contribute to the region as we know it today? In the institutional memories of several federal agencies, such as the Geological Survey and the Bureau of Reclamation, Powell appears as the inspiration behind their growth and presence in the region.[4] Most western historians go beyond such characterizations to describe Powell as an important social reformer, but all they usually mean is that he tried to increase the size of agricultural landholdings allowed under the government's homestead laws, in response to the western climate. Despite several good biographies of the man, and a thousand brief acknowledgments of his importance, Powell remains widely misunderstood. He is everybody's hero, the intrepid navigator of the West's most charismatic river, a paragon of rational, scientific planning, and so forth. But his most significant legacy remains obscure and even forgotten. That legacy was a set of ideas pertaining to the American people's relationship to the western lands, ideas that were more radical, more sweeping than we have appreciated or ever tried to apply. I want to retrieve them from neglect and ask what they still might offer us at this late date in the region's history.

But before examining those ideas, we must understand their background and trace the stages of Powell's education in the western landscape. It was an education obtained in the field, not the library, as almost all his education had been, and it focused on the land itself. Powell, as I have indicated, was a scientist, interested in such topics as geology, geomorphology, stream hydraulics, and climate. He was not really engaged by biology of any sort; the native grasses he trod on in going west, the stunning wildlife he saw, the new ideas of biological evolution floating in the air, did not really interest him. What seized his imagination was the inorganic. He sensed a compelling story in that realm, one that would reveal how the West had come to be what it was and would suggest to Americans what they needed to do if they were to make a successful civilization in the region. The western lands were not a blank slate on which any identity, old or new, could be arbitrarily written. One had to study what had occurred there before culture—any culture, Indian or European—had arrived. It was as a physical scientist, therefore, that Powell approached the latent region spreading before him.

Hitherto regions had emerged from a long folk process of people settling, gaining experience, adapting to the terrain. That had been so in Europe and Asia as it had been in North America. Both the North and the South of the United States had emerged before modern science had much influence over the popular mind, before the word *scientist* had even been coined. The American West would be different in part because it would take form in an age deeply impressed by science and would owe much of its identity to the work of scientists like Powell.

Going down the Colorado River in 1869 (and again two years later), Powell took his scientific mission seriously, even if it meant risking his men's displeasure. Although they soon lost most of the instruments they had packed in the boats, they had to stop repeatedly for observations. Powell continually sought places to stand in order to get an integrated, comprehensive view of the country. The book describing those voyages, *The Exploration of the Colorado River and Its Canyons*, set the pattern that he would follow throughout the voyage and indeed throughout his career. The first part of the book is a series of long views from on high, providing a systematic orientation to the entire Southwest before plunging the reader into the canyons, whipping through the rapids. Powell begins by describing the drainage pattern of the major rivers—the Green, the Grand, the Gila, the San Juan—and the placement of the mountains that are their source—the Wind River Range, the Uintas, the Front Range of the Rockies, San Francisco Peak. He points out other prominent landforms, including the Mogollon Escarpment, the Kaiparowits and Kaibab plateaus, the San Rafael Swell, the miscellany of cliffs and valleys. At one point he carries the reader to a grand vista on the Paunsagunt Plateau in southern Utah, nine thousand feet above sea level, to illustrate the elements at work in the landscape:

> Below me, to the southwest, I could look off into the canyons of the Virgen [sic] River, down into the canyon of the Kanab, and far away into the Grand Canyon of the Colorado. From the lowlands of the Great Basin and from the depths of the Grand Canyon clouds crept up over the cliffs and floated over the landscape below me, concealing the canyons and mantling the mountains and mesas and buttes; still on toward me the clouds rolled, burying the landscape in their progress, until at last the region below was covered by a mantle of storm—a tumultuous sea of rolling clouds, black and angry in parts, white as the

foam of the cataracts here and there, and everywhere flecked with resplendent sheen. Below me spread a vast ocean of vapor, for I was above the clouds. On descending to the plateau, I found that a great storm had swept the land, and the dry arroyos of the day before were the channels of a thousand streams of tawny water, born of the ocean of vapor which had invaded the land before my vision.[5]

Here he introduces the reader to the great central story of the West, the interplay of geophysical forces that had been working on the landscape over eons. In the rest of the book, as the river narration proceeds, he follows the same strategy. After a hard day of navigating through churning waters and eating an indifferent dinner cooked on the sandy shore, he liked to go climbing up the canyon walls. Leaving his boats and companions behind, with his sore stump hanging uselessly at his side, he struggled to the rim to see the terrain he was passing through. Sometimes the way up was more dangerous than he anticipated; once, in fact, he got trapped on a narrow ledge, unable to go up or down, and had to be rescued by another in the party. He learned to sit without fear or trembling on the very brink of a canyon, looking down several thousand feet, though it took years of such forced bravery to cool his nerves. What he sought in all that strenuous exercise was not thrills but scientific perspective. To a greater extent than any of his predecessors in western exploration, Powell tried to ask comprehensive questions about the whole of the place, about how it came to be what it was and how it was still taking form before his eyes.

Earlier explorers had made maps and catalogued the products of the country, but none of them had Powell's extraordinary synthesizing power. He was a masterful organizer of knowledge, concisely summing up what was known and indicating what remained to be studied. In his wake came other scientists, making maps, studying the region's geomorphology, measuring its stream-flow and erosion rates, collecting data on its drought cycles, looking for mineral wealth. Scientists in biology and ecology also came to study such topics as the migration patterns of whooping cranes or the salt-coping mechanisms of the region's vegetation. The pursuit of scientific knowledge about the West and its organization into general ideas were one of Powell's most important legacies, and as they went forward the region took on deeper and deeper meaning. The scientific exploration of this new region of the West did not begin or end with Powell, but he may have been its most important exponent.

Regions, to be sure, are based on something more than scientific definitions, even in the modern age. Other people came into the country too, people with no interest in science, and they were far more numerous than the explorer-scientists, including entrepreneurs, rural settlers, laborers, women as well as men, people of all races, people from every corner of the earth. All of them contributed to the meaning of the West. Consequently the region would never have a single comprehensive identity; despite Powell's hope, there is no single place to stand and take in the whole picture, the entire history, the full experience of many human beings. Western history today is rightly understood as requiring us to see the place from every angle of vision, including that of every race, class, and gender.

But the diverse peoples of the West have had something in common, too: a big, concrete, powerful landscape of rock, vapor, climate, and all its patterns of structure and process. A region may acquire many cultural meanings, as this one has, but it also has underlying physical realities that provide a unifying experience and a common set of challenges. As a scientist, Powell believed in the possibility of an objectively apprehended natural West. In struggling to the rim of the canyons, he was trying to overcome his own cultural bias, his own limitations, in order to see the land in and for itself. He then tried to show others who came into the place—Northerners, Southerners, Europeans, all kinds of immigrants—what that objective physical reality was. They needed, he thought, to know where they had arrived, and science would be their best guide.

Within a year following his first exploring trip down the Colorado, Powell was in charge of a congressionally authorized and funded scientific survey of the mountain West, including Colorado, New Mexico, and Utah. He went exploring overland across the entire Colorado Plateau, down to Albuquerque, into Arizona and Nevada, meeting frequently with the native peoples of the area and learning their languages. With remarkable speed he rose in Washington circles, until he was one of the most respected scientists in the government's employ. A decade after his first voyage, he was appointed to the Public Lands Commission, which undertook a general review of the settlement of the West, and thereby he learned more about the environment and the laws that had been made to exploit it. He was named director of the U.S. Geological Survey in 1881, the leading federal scientific agency at the time, an agency of central importance to western development. During all that time, from 1869 to 1881, Powell kept on striving for that comprehensive scientific vision of the West, and eventually he found it.

What made this region strikingly different from the eastern part of the

country, Powell concluded, was its aridity. "The eastern portion of the
United States," he wrote, "is supplied with abundant rainfall for agricultural purposes, receiving the necessary amount from the evaporation of
the Atlantic Ocean and the Gulf of Mexico; but westward the amount
of aqueous precipitation diminishes in a general way until at last a region
is reached where the climate is so arid that agriculture is not successful
without irrigation."[6] Powell based this generalization not only on his
own observations but also on a rain chart compiled in 1868 for the
Smithsonian Institution by Charles A. Shott, which showed that, aside
from a humid coastal strip north of San Francisco toward Seattle and a
few high mountain slopes, the West received less than twenty inches of
rainfall a year on average.[7] The chart showed also that a broad belt
separated that arid country from the eastern humid region—a "subhumid"
belt that covered most of Texas, Oklahoma, Kansas, and Nebraska, "a
beautiful prairie country throughout," covering 10 percent of the entire
United States exclusive of Alaska. The arid zone of the West was much
larger still, comprising 40 percent of the entire country. So altogether
the two major zones of the West, the arid and the subhumid, covered a
space that was quite as big as the East, beckoning to settlers tired of war,
eager for land of their own, but confronting them with a colossal set of
differences. The West would set rigorous new terms for their institutions
and traditions.

The wriggling isohyetal lines on the Smithsonian chart indicated at
once natural and cultural facts. They marked a major transition for
agriculture as well as rainfall (20 inches being the minimum required for
crops), and that agriculture was a cultural phenomenon. People invent
agriculture; that is, they choose some plants to eat, cultivating and
breeding them, while ignoring others. That is so of all the major
agricultural systems on which humans depend; whether they involve
wheat, sugar, corn, or rice, always they are cultural constructions. But
since food is plant and animal life, it is also part of nature. Food must
satisfy the body's physiological needs. The West, the isohyetals suggested, could not fill those needs over much of its extent, because it did
not have enough moisture. Outside a few oases, all of the foods cultivated
by people historically would have difficulty surviving there. That was a
natural fact, and no amount of dreaming or experimenting could alter it.
If people adapted their agricultural techniques and learned to raise food
in those oases, they could manage to live comfortably. Nature, in any
case, set the conditions for their success, and humans had no choice but
to accept them.

As a scientist impressed with the power of nature, Powell was to a point an environmental determinist: he assumed, that is, that any settlement of the region would be impossible without relying on agriculture as its core economic activity. He understood that nature determined, and had always determined, the essential style and scope of that agriculture. Unless Americans suddenly learned how to domesticate the native vegetation of the new region—sagebrush, Mormon tea, shadscale, cactus—and to eat their products, they were going to have to adapt.

Despite thousands of years of residence, and much intelligent trial-and-error experimentation, Indians had still not turned those native western plants into major foodstuffs, but had continued to rely on maize, pumpkins, and beans introduced from other parts of the hemisphere. Even then they found they could cultivate them in only a few favorable locations. One might argue that they had been trapped by their cultural heritage as much as confronted by nature's patterns of aridity, but to make that argument would be to assume that plant domestication is a completely open possibility. In fact agriculture is always the outcome of a limited intelligence working on the limited possibilities afforded by plant and animal genetics. Powell did not reason all those matters out explicitly, but he did know, as any scientist would know, that nature sets real, firm demands on the human species, so vitally dependent on water, protein, and minerals for its survival. That was a point of view, however, that many other Americans had not yet acquired.

If Powell found the unifying environmental reality of the West in aridity, he also came to understand the economic realities that were sweeping into the West, as they were sweeping across the entire nation, in the 1870s. Men of wealth and power were everywhere looking for resources to exploit, putting into their private pockets as much as they could grasp. They were claiming railroad rights-of-way, mineral deposits, timber stands, all the grasslands in the public domain, and most critical for the long-term development of the West, the scarce water resources. Americans lacking comparable means or avidity or shrewdness were quickly being shut out of the picture. Powell sensed that the new region would not be theirs if economic trends persisted. "If in the eagerness for present development," he warned, "a land and water system shall grow up in which the practical control of agriculture shall fall into the hands of water companies, evils will result therefrom that generations may not be able to correct, and the very men who are now lauded as benefactors to the country will, in the ungovernable reaction which is sure to come, be denounced as oppressors of the people."[8]

Powell was not a naive primitivist who looked on the West as an escape from the emerging modern life of the East. He believed enthusiastically in the idea of progress, and he wanted to see progress come westward, advancing into the very canyonlands he had explored, making tame whatever was wild. As the means to progress, he accepted the private business corporation, along with modern technology, the industrial revolution, and science. But he did not want to see concentrated private interests completely rule the West, as they were already ruling the East, turning the defeated southern states into their subjects, as they had long ago done to northern farmers. Powell wanted to see the West make progress in a different direction, toward a future securely placed in the hands of a self-governing agrarian population, men and women who were progressive in their thinking but not so intensely capitalistic in their motives. The challenge, as he saw it, was to save the West before it was permanently lost. If science could reveal the structure of the natural environment, perhaps it could also suggest a better social order for the region.

Powell's *Report on the Lands of the Arid Region,* published in 1878, provided a preliminary sketch of that social order. A familiar document to most western historians, its central theme is that the Land Ordinance of 1785 had to be scrapped, along with the whole system of transferring the public domain to private ownership. The Ordinance had established a national land survey, the township-and-range system, that divided the country from the Appalachian Mountains to the Pacific Coast into a rigid grid of square parcels one mile on a side, subdivided into quarter sections of 160 acres. Scientific though it once had seemed in its geometrical and mathematical precision, it disregarded all evidence from the earth sciences about the diversity of the country. As the survey approached the subhumid, then the arid region, it would prove more and more inadequate. Settlers who selected a homestead from that grid might find themselves living on a barren mesa, with no surface water at all or, conversely, locating on a well-watered, well-wooded bottomland with more acres than they could cultivate. Powell called on Congress to go back to the old, discarded metes-and-bounds system that had been applied east of the Appalachians and that had allowed property lines to follow the natural distribution of resources. If that system had worked well enough for centuries in Europe and for a long time in the coastal East, then it might work in the West too—it might even work *better* in that highly irregular landscape, extraordinarily complex in its landforms though simple in aridity.

Powell did propose an important new wrinkle in the old metes-and-bounds system to meet the regional exigencies. He would have the federal government make a prior classification of all land before letting settlers in to claim it and mark out their boundaries. Scientists would be put in charge of deciding which lands should be open for irrigation, which should be kept as timberlands, and which should be classed as grazing lands, never to be plowed up for crops. By indicating those three categories on maps, scientists could guide ordinary people lacking much experience to the places where they had the best chance to make a living. They would learn in advance where they might find sufficient water and where they must get along without it. Under the Ordinance system, in contrast, the West was fast becoming a vast, chaotic lottery in which only a few profited.

The rest of Powell's recommendations of 1878 are also rather well known. He would scrap the entire body of homestead and preemption legislation. He would allow only two types of private land tenure in the West: small irrigated farms no larger than 80 acres, all gathered together into irrigation districts; and large "pasturage farms," or livestock ranches, no larger than 2,560 acres, likewise organized into grazing districts. Every individual landowner would thus be bound to his neighbors in a collective unit. All other lands would remain in federal ownership, though the timber or mineral resources on them might be sold or given to private entrepreneurs. All the water would belong to those who owned the land; no one could control any water who did not possess an irrigated or pasturage farm. Instead of a monopoly over scarce resources exercised by a few capitalists, Powell envisioned a region permanently put into the hands of the rural many, bound together in a common body politic, like a school of fish swimming together to defend themselves against sharks.

Powell published those reform proposals in 1878, and nothing came of them. Neither Congress nor the public heeded his recommendations. The General Land Office continued to follow the Ordinance system, with its abstract geometrical approach to the land. The typical homestead patented under the system remained for a long while the standard eastern 160-acre parcel, though eventually that size was increased somewhat for stockraisers. All those facts are common knowledge among western historians and have been pointed out repeatedly. What has not been said is that, following Powell's initial failure to get his ideas adopted, he worked them over into an even more radical shape, until by 1890 he had arrived at a master plan for the West that has never been sufficiently understood.

In the early months of that year, Major Powell ("Professor" would suit him better, for he had never lost his didactic style) ran a seminar for politicians and the public on understanding the West. The House Select Committee on Irrigation of Arid Lands in the United States held hearings during February and March on a bill "to cede the arid lands to the States and Territories wherein they are situate and to provide for irrigation and protection of forest lands and pasture lands." As the foremost authority on those lands, Powell repeatedly came to testify, each time bringing new maps to place on the wall before the congress-men. He intended to teach them, valley by valley, the logic of the western landscape and to suggest how a whole new political structure might be based on that logic. His first map was of the Rio Grande, from its headwaters in Colorado to El Paso, Texas. Then on another day he came with a map of the entire West, all 1,340,000 square miles of it; then a map of regional coal fields, of the major timberlands and the minor scrub forests (colored in contrasting shades of green), of the upper Arkansas River basin, of the Colorado River basin, of the Snake and the Bear, of . . . but there he ended abruptly, in the middle of March, indicating that he was prepared to discuss every watershed in the West, but was afraid he might exhaust the committee's patience with his passion for details.[9]

Powell wanted the congressmen to know the country as he knew it, both from high up on the canyon rim and down there on the river, and to understand its patterns of water, climate, and geology that had been interacting over so many eons. He wanted them to realize how little of the country could ever grow crops; at most there was water available for irrigating 100 million acres, a mere one out of nine acres, and that would require a considerable investment in storage reservoirs, of which there had been next to none by 1890. He wanted the men in the hearing room to appreciate the conflicts that were already brewing in those western valleys, as upstream developers diverted the water that downstream farmers had depended on, in the case of the Rio Grande Valley, for over a hundred years. Above all, he wanted them to see that all the natural resources of the West were connected into a single integrated whole, so that what was done to the mountain forests affected the lowland streams, and the lands without water were intricately related to those with water.

The Indians and Hispanos who had settled the country seemed to have understood well that environmental interrelatedness, but the Anglos did not. They came as possessive individuals pursuing private dreams, trying to fence in their portion of the whole. They failed to see how their lives were related to the lives of their neighbors, or how their lands depended on all the other lands in the vicinity. That was the root problem of the American West. The land had a complex unity that had evolved over time; however, the white settlers thought about the land, as they thought about each other, in simplifying, fragmenting terms and, consequently, would come to grief.

Take, for instance, the Arkansas River Valley, from its headwaters near Leadville, Colorado, to the Kansas line. Settlers on the lower stretch ignored at their peril what happened at the headwaters. If they wanted to survive, they must safeguard the forests growing there from wasteful fires, both to preserve a catchment for their water supply and to provide a source of wood. "Their homes are to be made, their farms are to be fenced, and their firewood is to be obtained from them." Nor could they afford to ignore the surrounding plains, whose best use was for grazing their livestock. "All of this land," Powell argued, "must by some means or other be placed under the control of these farmers. . . . If the water, the timber, and the grass are to be utilized and protected from destruction— and all of the values inhering in them are liable to destruction to a greater or less extent by mismanagement—then these people who are interested therein should have control and management of the unoccupied lands as a body-politic, and should be allowed to make their own rules and regulations for its protection and use."[10] There at last in Professor Powell's seminar was set forth the political system required by the logic of the landscape: a system of governance to achieve environmental conservation, democratic decisionmaking, and community stability.

Powell was arguing, in effect, that he did not think it wise to cede any part of the public domain to the states and allow them to dispose of it as they pleased, which is what many western congressmen wanted to do. That would only further complicate an already difficult situation caused by a set of political boundaries that made no environmental sense. Instead Powell would create a completely new set of governmental units (to augment, not replace, the state and county governments), based on what he called "hydrographic basins," or watersheds, reaching from one divide to another. "My theory," he explained, "is to organize in the United States another unit of government for specific purposes, for agriculture by irrigation, for the protection of the forests which are being destroyed by fire, and for the utilization of the pasturage which can only be utilized in large bodies; that is, to create a great body of common- wealths. In the main these commonwealths would be like county communities in the States." Powell had plotted on his maps the outlines

of 140 such units in the West, though he thought another ten or so might
be added, each of them approximately the size of two average counties.
Some of the new units would cross state lines. Within each unit a small
part of the land would be private property, mainly the irrigated farms, but
much would be held as communal lands—particularly the dry grasslands
and the mountain forests. Title to them would remain in federal hands,
but the local people would have the use of them and would make rules
for their management. "If they want that timber destroyed, if they want
to sell it, if they want to destroy it and wipe out irrigation, they are
responsible for it, and let them do as they please."[11]

Let them do as they please? The "them" in Powell's new West would
not be the "them" of laissez-faire America, where individuals were
expected to pursue their self-interest in disregard of others. Powell
wanted settlers to come together and make collective decisions about the
land. He wanted every settler to be involved in that process, and every
settler to have an equal share of the earth and an equal voice in its
disposition.

The label he gave those resource-planning and governing units,
"commonwealths," was a term originating in seventeenth-century
England, suggesting a sense of public good or welfare. Although it had
been carried to the American colonies and, at the time of the Revolution, had become part of the title of such states as Massachusetts,
Pennsylvania, and Virginia, it had faded from common usage. Now
revived by the government's top scientist, the idea of commonwealth
became modern, western, and environmental.

A few weeks after Powell finished his testimony before the House
committee, *Century Magazine* published a series of three articles by him,
presenting the same environmental analysis and political blueprint to
the American public. In the last of them, "Institutions for the Arid
Lands," Powell acknowledged that he had been influenced by Spanish
settlements in the Southwest and by the Mormons of Utah, who had
effectively communalized their natural resources. The beauty of those
models, in his eyes, was that they put power in the hands of local
communities. He emphatically rejected the alternative, already being
debated, of giving the federal government active, centralized control
over western resources. The government should not cede its lands to the
states, he felt, but neither should it set up a national administration to
guard the forests (it would soon become "a hotbed of corruption") nor an
irrigation administration to finance water development. The Spanish
and Mormon models demonstrated that local community control would,

in the long run, do more to educate people in stewardship of the earth, prevent large disparities of wealth, and be more efficient and economical. But again the vital element in those models was that they must subordinate the individual landowner to the decisions of the group. Local control must be truly communitarian.

In that same year of Professor Powell's seminar on the West, 1890, the Census Bureau announced the end of the frontier. The population of the seventeen western states and territories had reached 6,451,000, and the number was so large and so spread out that there was no longer a single discernible line of advancing settlement. The biggest city in the region was San Francisco, with 298,000 inhabitants, but there were other sizable urban centers, including Denver (107,000), Los Angeles (50,000), Salt Lake City (45,000), and Seattle (43,000).[12] Many of those cities had first been established as supply centers for the various mining or timber rushes into the West, beginning in California in 1848. Mining interests had long been engaged in staking out claims to the public domain, and under the Mining Law of 1872, they had solidified their right to "free and open" access to that land; in return they paid no royalties, tolerated little oversight, and went just about wherever they pleased. The region had long been their oyster. Powell did not explain how their legally guaranteed and highly individualistic freedom could be reconciled with his commonwealths and the principle of collective resource management. Would miners be shut out altogether, or would they have to negotiate access to minerals or water with powerful local organizations completely dominated by agriculturists? Powell did not address those questions nor indicate what voice those growing cities and towns would have in a system controlled by landowning farmers. Would the inhabitants of Santa Fe or Salt Lake City be able to participate in the new units of government? As presented his commonwealth idea had a strictly rural bias in a region that was already urban and industrial to a degree and fast becoming more so.[13]

The region would develop further in agricultural terms too, notwithstanding the census announcement regarding the frontier. Over the next three decades, more land would be taken up by homesteaders than in the previous three decades. From that perspective Powell was not too late when it came to reforming agricultural institutions. But was he too late when he called for dividing the West into 150 *agrarian* commonwealths?

The record does not show that anyone in the nation expressed much positive interest in Powell's recommendations, or even that there was any serious critical response that might have raised hard questions and forced him to work out the problems he had overlooked. The House committee listened to him politely but took no action, and whatever response the *Century* articles got is not recorded for posterity. Apparently, from the lack of any contrary evidence, we can say that the nation did not give them much thought at all, perhaps because they flew in the face of well-established institutions, and more seriously, in the face of a national culture of economic individualism. Homesteaders continued to come looking for a piece of land they could fence and manage on their own. The powerful lobbies for western development, on the other hand, led by railroad corporations, mining companies, cattle outfits invading the public domain, and the like, could not have seen much merit in so many commonwealths getting in their way.

Four years after offering his reforms, Powell resigned from the directorship of the Geological Survey, ostensibly because of the continuing pain from his wound, but in truth he was driven out of office by budget cuts and general indifference as much as by opposition to his ideas. Henceforth he devoted his days to anthropology and philosophy. In 1902 he died of a cerebral hemorrhage at his summer house on the coast of Maine, far from the West he had come to know better than anyone else of his generation.

Immediately following Powell's death, there were many touching testimonials by his Washington friends, associates, and protégés. They commonly extolled his career as a federal bureaucrat, his contributions to science in general (particularly to ethnography), his kindness to the younger men he drew into government service. Often they emphasized the contrast between his early humble background, his lack of formal education, and the international reputation he enjoyed at the time of his death. Daniel Coit Gilman, the president of Johns Hopkins University, remembered him "presiding over a meeting of the American Association for the Advancement of Science in Boston, where, attracted by his many endearing qualities and particularly by his genial manner, many men became his friends." Alexander Chamberlain of Clark University believed that "the monument of Major Powell is the Bureau of Ethnology," which studied the origin and culture of the American Indian. William Healey Dall, in an obituary read before the Philosophical Society of Washington, similarly concluded that Powell's contributions "to the understanding of the Indian, though largely developed through other workers, are his best gift to the store of modern science and that upon which his scientific reputation will chiefly rest." Gilbert Grosvener of the National Geographic Society wrote that "the public will probably always remember Major Powell most prominently for his dramatic exploration of the Grand Canyon of the Colorado." Almost uniquely among the memorialists, William Brewer of Yale recalled that Powell had been "a powerful advocate of reform in laws affecting the permanent welfare of the West," but he did not say what that reform was about. These men were generally Easterners who had known the Major as a figure in government, as a leader in scientific societies, or as a dinner companion, but they were not really interested in Powell as a conceptualist of the West or as an environmental reformer.[14]

Even some of Powell's most informed friends, his closest associates, either downplayed his political reformism or did not quite grasp what he had in mind. William M. Davis, for example, understood the National Reclamation Act, passed in 1902, just a short while before Powell died, to be a triumphant vindication of his senior's campaign to promote irrigation in the West. Much later a Michigan geologist imagined Powell lying sick up there in Maine, being "greatly cheered" on hearing the news of that congressional action. No less a friend than Grove Karl Gilbert, fellow geologist, coauthor of the 1878 *Report on the Arid Lands*, claimed that Powell had been the inspiration and genius behind the act. Early on Powell had pushed for irrigation, he recalled, at a time when other Americans believed that the West would be a natural garden of productivity. Despite much hostile criticism of that recommendation, a general movement "for the intelligent development of the West" had eventually followed Powell's lead, "a movement whose latest achievement is the so-called reclamation law."[15]

All those observers completely missed the distinctive point of Powell's approach to irrigation. The reclamation act, which had been drawn up and promoted by Senator Francis Newlands of Nevada and vigorously supported by President Theodore Roosevelt, had little to do with Powell's self-reliant, self-governing commonwealths. The act federalized western water development by placing the income from the sale of lands into a reclamation fund and using it to build dams and canals in the region. A federal office, the Reclamation Service (later renamed the Bureau of Reclamation) was set up to administer the program, an outcome Powell had feared and explicitly criticized: "I say to the Government: Hands off! Furnish the people with institutions of justice, and let them do the work for themselves." Any dams or canals should be built with local money or funds borrowed from capitalists, he insisted, not with federal dollars, federal authority, or federal control.

Why did even Powell's friends not quite see, or perhaps not quite share, his commonwealth vision? Why was is it so quickly buried in the archives of the past? His friends were generally not captives of the economic individualism that was rampant out West; on the contrary, they tended to be strong institutionalists, forming clubs and societies, holding positions in distinguished universities, or devoting their lives to government service. The key to the puzzle, I think, is that they were institutionalists in the East, not the West, and they were national institutionalists, not regionalists. The institutions they wanted to build up were eastern universities, eastern academic societies, and above all, eastern institutions in government. They were proponents of an active federal response to national problems. Sometimes, though rarely, they thought about the West, but then they came to different conclusions than Powell. The West must serve the national interest, they felt, an interest defined by Easterners in terms of wealth, power, social harmony, and national economic longevity.

Powell, in contrast, thought about the West in regional, not national terms. He may have lived in Washington, devoting much of his adult life to federal projects, but when it came to planning for the West, he stood with the folk at the grass roots, asking what was in *their* best long-term interest. It was not a perspective others around him shared; they must have looked on many of his regionalist ideas as "unrealistic" or quaint and soon cast them into obscure shadows.

The leading figures in burying Powell's political ideas were President Theodore Roosevelt and his chief forester, Gifford Pinchot, who dominated Washington thinking about the West and its natural resources during the first decade of the twentieth century. For Roosevelt the great issue of the day was to make the American nation-state the dominant force on the earth, greater than England, Germany, Japan, or Russia had ever been or ever would be. America must be first in industry, military might, population, and moral influence. The most important means to that end, he repeated over and over, was a national program of conserving natural resources, putting an end to the destruction of forests, to the abusive, haphazard or limited development of rivers, and to the depletion of vital raw materials. A chapter in his autobiography, "The Natural Resources of the Nation," sets forth the major aspects of that program; he boasts of his role in getting the Reclamation Act passed, of setting up the Forest Service, of bringing millions of acres under federal management.[16] The point of all those efforts was to promote a nationalist instead of an individualist or even a local communitarian ethos.[17]

In the last year of his presidency, Roosevelt assembled a National

Conservation Commission in Washington and in his opening remarks told them, "Your task is to make the nation's future as great as its present. That is what the conservation of our resources means." Again he argued that conservation "is the bottom round of the ladder on our upward progress toward a condition in which the nation as a whole, and its citizens as individuals, will set national efficiency and the public welfare before personal profit." The chairman of the commission was Gifford Pinchot, and he explained to the others that conservation "expresses a deep-seated national conviction, latent until it came, that we have inherited from our forefathers both an opportunity for ourselves and duty to those who come after us. Conservation demands the use of common prudence and common foresight in dealing with the great material resources upon which our present and future welfare depends."[18] In Pinchot's moral imagination, as in Roosevelt's, there was a strong sense that the common good must take precedence over private self-interest, but both men defined that good in nationalistic terms. Both looked to a few leaders in Washington to determine what that good should be, and both men subordinated the West to their nationalist, indeed imperialist, hopes.

The most elaborate expression of the Rooseveltian philosophy was the book *The Promise of American Life*, published by the New York editor Herbert Croly in the same year as the National Conservation Commission's report. The book was a forceful critique of laissez-faire economics and a reasoned demand that centralized state power be encouraged to give direction to a nation in drift. Croly especially admired the nation's first Secretary of the Treasury, Alexander Hamilton, for his idea of "energetic and intelligent assertion of national power," though he wanted to see that power serve the needs of all the people, not just Hamilton's elite business class. But Croly's "new nationalism" was also a repudiation of any competing ways of discovering the common good. Like Roosevelt and Pinchot, he assumed that there was one such good, a national good, and that the best people must be brought into the federal government and given the full means to discover and achieve it. Croly does not mention the West at all in his book, nor the name of John Wesley Powell, nor does he consider that the good of a people living in a remote western river valley might conflict with the good of the nation-state.[19]

Another label we commonly attach to this Roosevelt-Pinchot-Croly school of thinking is Progressivism, a movement emerging from within the Republican party at the turn of the century but leaving a profound impact on American politics generally. According to George Mowry, one of the movement's leading historians, Progressivism involved a "worship of the strong man," melded with "the ethics of the social gospel." It promised to bring "strong good men" into government to protect morality and pursue progress. "They were ambitious men and ruthless, but only ruthless in their zeal for human advancement."[20] Progressivism created, among its many accomplishments, the first national conservation movement, which has left a deep impression on the whole country, but especially the American West. The essential theme of Progressive conservation was, in Samuel Hays's words, "rational planning to promote efficient development and use of all natural resources." Who should decide the means and ends of that planning? Not the people of the West, Hays makes clear, nor their elected representatives. "Since resource matters were basically technical in nature, . . . technicians, rather than legislators, should deal with them. Foresters should determine the desirable annual timber cut; hydraulic engineers should establish the feasible extent of multiple-purpose river development, and the specific location of reservoirs; agronomists should decide which forage areas could remain open for grazing without undue damage to water supplies."[21]

The implications in those ideas for the West were profound. Since that region was still largely in the public domain, it offered the best opportunity for good strong men, filled with moral idealism and technical expertise, to come out from Washington and show what they could do to achieve the common good. They were men imbued, writes Hays, with "the technological spirit," which accepts the conquest of nature as humankind's highest goal, but they wanted to put themselves in charge of the conquest.

John Wesley Powell was, to a point, one of them—but not wholly so. Although he was full of the technological spirit, he stopped short of the federal technocratic ideal promoted by Roosevelt and his supporters. Powell would give plenty of advice to western communities, but then he would leave the final decisions up to the people who must live most directly with the results of their resource management or mismanagement. He did not consider how western forests or rivers might make the American nation great among the nations of the world; rather, he thought of what resources might contribute to the stability of small communities. Like the Progressives, he had no use for impatient western entrepreneurs who wanted immediate access to the sources of personal wealth. He looked beyond the gratification of the individual and the present generation. Unlike the Progressives, however, he did not look much beyond the local. So he became irrelevant to an age of reformers who had their eyes on grander goals.

Powell's reputation fell into general neglect from his death until the year 1931, when a Texas historian rediscovered him and, heavily influenced by his writings, developed a theory of western exceptionalism. Walter Prescott Webb opened his landmark text, *The Great Plains*, with a quotation from one of Powell's magazine articles: "The industries of the West are necessarily unlike those of the East[;] . . . a new phase of Aryan civilization is being developed in the western half of America." Later in the book, he devoted several pages to presenting Powell's land reforms of 1878, dealing with such regional innovations as irrigation and pasturage farms. Of course those reforms had been intended mainly for the "arid region" to the west, not for the subhumid zone of the Great Plains, but they supported Webb's notion that the United States was not a seamless whole and that each region must follow its own course.[22]

Since Webb is where the modern regional history of the American West begins, it is important to see his history as a legacy of Powell. At long last the Major was beginning to find an audience, and it came among a rising generation of western regionalists. The process of discovering the West that had begun right after the Civil War had long been stymied by capitalist economic expansion and Progressive political thought, both antiregionalist in their loyalties, but now it was back on track, gathering new energy from the sight of a nation floundering in the economic doldrums of the Great Depression.

Webb, however, misunderstood Powell almost as badly as the federal reclamationists did. He blamed the failure of adaptive land reforms on the recalcitrance of eastern lawyers and politicians: the reforms "fitted too well the needs of the West," he wrote, "to get adequate consideration in the East, where the laws for the West were made." That was poppycock; it was mainly western politicians who blocked Powell's reforms, because they would have prevented private interests from getting control of resources and forced people into a collective pattern of settlement. Webb accepted Powell's exceptionalist argument, but he missed his communitarian principle, which neither the West nor the East found attractive.

The Great Depression was also the time of the Dust Bowl and of reappraisal of conventional thinking about the West. Powell's name began to pop up repeatedly, including among some government planners who blamed the dust storms on a failure in agricultural adaptation and recalled some of his ideas. But prominent western politicians seemed to

have forgotten him completely, even those who had become conservationists. In 1934, for example, Congressman Edward Taylor of Colorado
finally pushed through a long-overdue reform of grazing practices on the
public lands, which had been virtually free and unsupervised. "We are
rapidly permitting the creations of small Sahara Deserts in every one of
our Western States today," he warned his fellow legislators. The Taylor
Grazing Act organized stockmen into rule-making local districts, an idea
that may seem like a recognizably Powellian solution. Yet nowhere in the
debate over that act did Taylor or any other politician remember that
Powell had been there before them, that he had advocated a communal
grazing arrangement as part of his commonwealth idea. Taylor in fact
seemed to think that his remedy was merely an extension of Progressive
conservation. "We of the West," he declared, "have slowly and reluc-
tantly come to see the importance and the wisdom of Theodore Roosevelt's
and Governor Pinchot's policy and the foresight of the conservation
sentiment of the country." What he indicated in that confession was that
he, along with other Westerners, had come to accept the Progressives'
judgment that the West was not yet ready to assume responsibility for the
public lands; they still required the federal government's close supervision over their self-destructive habits.[23]

Outside of government, however, other Westerners besides Webb had
begun to rediscover Powell and honor him for having clearly seen the
environmental realities of the region. The Montana newspaperman
Joseph Kinsey Howard, for instance, referred to the 1878 report as "one
of the most remarkable studies of social and economic forces ever written
in America." Had it been followed, he thought, it would have prevented
the inevitable ruin of the northern plains by greed and prevented the
blasting of so many naive hopes; "it would have been cheaper to listen to
J. W. Powell."[24] A similar argument was made in 1950 by Henry Nash
Smith, in his book *Virgin Land*, where Powell appears as a heroic realist
opposed by such dangerous fantasists as Ferdinand V. Hayden, Samuel
Aughey, and Charles Dana Wilber (who promised settlers that rain
would follow the plow), Horace Greeley, Frederick Jackson Turner, and
a host of strident western boosters. Powell, writes Smith, demanded that
"the West should submit to rational and scientific revision of its central
myth [of the fertile garden] and indeed that the nation at large should
yield one of the principal underpinnings of its faith in progress, in the
mission of America, in manifest destiny."[25]

By the mid-twentieth century, Powell had made a full second coming,
thanks to Webb, Howard, and Smith, and to a new series of biographical

studies that followed. The first of them was published in 1951 by William Culp Darrah, who pointed out that he had begun his rediscovery of Powell twenty years earlier, through an interest in the nineteenth-century debate over Darwinism. Darrah's book was a careful biography of the man and his life that drew on nearly sixty-five hundred items from institutions all over the country.[26] In the very next year, Paul Meadows brought out a shorter study of "the intellectual life of the man," suggested to him by Joseph Kinsey Howard. "The Major does not deserve the obscurity which the half-century since his death has brought him," Meadows wrote; he was "a conservationist out of time."[27]

But the most important milestone in the reawakening of interest in Powell was the publication in 1954 of what remains today the best book ever done on the man, and one of the most important books ever written about the region: Wallace Stegner's *Beyond the Hundredth Meridian: John Wesley Powell and the Second Opening of the West.* It, too, had been suggested by an older mentor, in this case by Bernard DeVoto, who like Stegner was a native son of Utah and a leader in a new western regionalism. For both men the long neglect of Powell was part of a general dismissal of the West as a subject for serious historical attention. The hold of Turner's frontier thesis over the American mind, which did not describe conditions in the West, and the hold of romantic mythologizing, which reduced the West to a land of adventure and nothing more, were to blame for that neglect. Though neither DeVoto nor Stegner put the argument so boldly, what they were clearly calling for was a new understanding of the significance of the West, one that made Powell central: the West as a battleground between the global economic system of capitalism, which was amenable neither to environmental adaptation, conservation, nor democracy, and an alternative social ideal of public planning, communal ownership of resources, and community decisionmaking about their development. In Stegner's own words, "within the bureaucrat dwelt a democratic idealist with a peculiarly unselfish and devoted notion of public service. And both the bureaucrat and the idealist knew that private interests, whether they dealt in cattle or sheep, oil, minerals, coal, timber, water, or land itself, could not be trusted or expected to take care of the land or conserve its resources for the use of future generations."[28]

So Powell at last had his appreciators, and a brilliant group of them at that, with as much talent as the Major himself and as firm a commitment to the West. Yet even the best of them, Wallace Stegner, was too eager to honor Powell's achievement by claiming that his ideas had triumphed

in the modern era. Supposedly Powell had been the precursor of the
welfare state in America, of Franklin Roosevelt's New Deal, of federal
planning in the West, of the Forest Service, the Park Service, the Grazing
Service (later the Bureau of Land Management), and the Bureau of
Reclamation. Powell, it was claimed, would have approved those agencies' stewardship of the public lands. "On any composite map showing
the modern use and management and reclamation of western lands,"
declared Stegner, "it would appear as if almost every suggestion Powell
made has been finally adopted, and every kind of western land is being
put to the kind of use Powell advocated."[29] Well, there was considerable
truth to that claim; the federal land agencies had in fact put their
expertise to conscientious use and had moved toward a more scientifically enlightened management. But that same composite map of the
West would not show 140 or 150 new units of government, those
commonwealths that Powell wanted and thought were vital to democracy, nor would it show that any of the land-use adjustments had been
achieved by local people acting in their own long-term collective
interest. The vital element from Powell's point of view was missing.
Stegner, in effect, had rescued Powell from oblivion only by making him
over into the fountainhead of Progressive conservation in the West, the
patron saint of federalized management. Arrayed against that Powell
legacy, as he told it, were the indefatigable private interests, the land-
grabbers, reasserting themselves once more in the Eisenhower years, with
their man Douglas "Give-away" McKay presiding over the Department
of the Interior. To defeat those interests, Stegner, DeVoto, and conservationists in general had lined up with the federal ideal, even dragging
Powell with them for legitimacy and authority.

Every age writes not only history but also biography to address its own
agenda. We cannot escape that bias toward making the past relevant. We
can, however, be careful of enlisting the dead in causes or movements
that they neither anticipated nor understood. We can try to approach
them in their own terms, then ask what is useful or not so useful in those
terms today. Trying to follow that principle here, I cannot find in John
Wesley Powell anywhere an imprimatur for the public-lands system we
have created in the American West today, for federal construction
agencies like the Bureau of Reclamation, or for the U.S. Forest Service.
Nor for that matter can I find any validation for modern environmental
groups like the Sierra Club, the Wilderness Society, or Earth First! or,
conversely, for any Sagebrush Rebellion, "wise-use" movement, or
states-rights ideology as expressed by recent western land-grabbers and

politicians. The debate over the region's environment has changed radically in the nearly full century since Powell's death, and we will never know just how or whether the Major would have changed with the times.

Westerners of many stripes want to lay claim to Powell, because they sense that he shared their interest in, their loyalty toward, the West. He was, in a sense, the father of their country. But today he would be a most bewildered old fellow if he came back to look at the West we have been making: a West that is now the home of 77 million people, ranging from Korean shopowners in Los Angeles to African-American college students in Las Vegas, from Montana novelists and poets to Colorado trout fishermen and skiers, from Kansas buffalo ranchers to Utah prison guards.[30] How to make a regional whole of all that? And how turn the life and ideas of a nineteenth-century frontier dirt farmer become explorer-geologist become environmental reformer into a prophet for all those people today?

What those 77 million still have in common, despite the demographic and cultural changes, is the land itself. Even today questions about how that land ought to be used, exploited, or preserved continue to dominate western conversations and public-policy debates. Much of that land is still in public title, despite all the access that has been allowed to private users. Perhaps the most distinctive feature of the West, after aridity, is the fact of extensive public ownership of that land, hundreds of millions of acres in all, a feature that ties the past to the present. In New Mexico the federal government owns 33 percent of the state, in Utah 64 percent, in Nevada 82 percent, though in my own state of Kansas it owns about 1 percent.[31]

Some persist in trying to alter that situation to their advantage. In 1979 the Nevada legislature passed a resolution demanding transfer of federal lands to the states, ostensibly to give local people greater control of their own destiny—allowing them to decide what should be wilderness and what should not, or how many cows a family can graze in its neighborhood and how many mines a company can dig—though the whole nation understood that the real, controlling purpose behind that resolution was to give entrepreneurs more freedom to develop land and make money. The resolution failed, as did the movement to abolish the federal domain in the West.

The western public lands are simply not going to pass into private ownership ever. Slowly but irreversibly, the nation and the region are moving in a direction that other nations took a long while back, toward placing more and more rules and restrictions on the rights of individuals to develop any land, public or private. We are moving toward communalizing land in America, though slowly and with much litigation, more slowly often than the developers are moving to turn it into shopping malls and housing estates. Any one who resists that trend is fighting a lost cause. Because of that general cultural movement, much of the West will remain in public ownership. It is far easier to apply rules and restrictions on development when land is already in public ownership, and that is why the West will have to live under federal title for a long time to come.

Westerners, however, would feel much better about this trend if the main locus of decisionmaking moved closer to home. So would Americans in other regions; very few people in the eastern states, I suspect, would want their lands communalized under strong federal control, or even under the control of the states. Here is the point where John Wesley Powell, the Powell of history rather than of myth, as nearly as I can discern him, may have some useful suggestions to make. Remember his commonwealths organized along watersheds, stretching laterally from divide to divide, encompassing the lowlands and the highlands, including all the key renewable resources the land has to offer. Does that idea still have any possibilities in the West of today? Can some part of it be revived and institutionalized? Can it offer inspiration to the old North and South, where the main problem is to recreate a public space where so much land has been privatized for so long?

Powell's alternative model of the body politic would have been composed of all the farm owners living within each hydrographic basin, including private and public lands, all managed as a single, integrated unit. That is obviously not an adequate base for democracy in the West today, where only a tiny minority of the population own any significant acreage (in California, to take an extreme example, agriculturists constitute less than 1 percent). Massive urbanization has left most Westerners with no direct relationship to the land or the natural world that supports them, yet they too have a stake in how the land fares. Powell's commonwealths could not call themselves democratic if they left out that majority of the people, but including them in a meaningful way, as informed, capable, interested participants in land- and water-use decisions, will not be easy.

The fact of the matter is that they *are* left out today, more left out then ever before. Whenever Bureau of Land Management officials sit down with their lessees, Bureau of Reclamation officials with their water clients, Forest Service officials with timber executives, or any of the above with lawyers from the leading environmental organizations, the vast majority of Westerners are left out. Most decisions made about the land today are not made by the people as a whole, or any approximation of them, but by a small elite who may or may not represent the public interest. So Powell's commonwealths, which might still be easy enough to draw on a map, must face the dilemma that all institutions today confront: how to enable all people—farm workers as well as farm owners, racial minorities as well as majorities, the illiterate as well as the informed—a voice in and responsibility for the decisions that affect their lives and the lives of their children. Powell gave us an outline of environmental democracy, but only we can adapt it and make it real for this age.

Another change has come to the West over the last century, a growing awareness that the region holds treasures of natural beauty and biological diversity that should be preserved against all threats of development or use. The national parks and wildlife refuges of the region, the greatest anywhere in the world, express that awareness, however haltingly. I cannot find in Powell anywhere, not even in his commonwealth idea, any room for that awareness. Had such treasures been given over to irrigation communities, what would have been their fate? The history of the West strongly suggests that rural landowners have been among the slowest to accept the need for ecological preservation. Their notion of conservation, if and where it exists, is to preserve the capacity of the watershed or the soil or the forest to furnish resources for their future consumption—and often that is all. Perhaps broadening the electorate included in those commonwealths, as suggested above, bringing into the decision process more urban environmentalists, backpackers, campers, and hunters, would broaden the conservation ethic implied in Powell's scheme. But the problem is not merely one of narrow views needing more enlightenment. Local communities cannot be *expected* to bear all the economic burdens of saving wildlife, wilderness, Yosemite Valley, or the Grand Canyon; such work is necessarily the responsibility of a larger population, of the nation as a whole, of the world, indeed of the human species.

Despite its several weaknesses, its inability to anticipate all the conditions and issues that characterize the American West of the late twentieth century, Powell's alternative model for governing the region is still capable of being made relevant. It is still possible, though getting more difficult all the time, to bring all citizens into the process of decisionmaking for the public lands and the natural environment as a whole. The issue, as before, is whether we have the desire to do so. Such a move has much to recommend it. It might improve people's under-standing of and responsibility for the physical world that supports them. It might offer a post-Progressive direction in conservation, opening a way out of the old cowboy capitalists versus federal bureaucrats confrontation that has for so long dominated western politics. It might allow a more distinctively regional culture to grow out of the great brown land.

Nearly a century after Powell's death, we are still discovering the West, still exploring its hidden country and mapping its physical reali-ties. We have not yet invented all the institutions we will ever need in order to live in the place. That is why Powell is still worth heeding. He is somewhere behind us in the canyons of the past, yet we can still catch the echo of his vision: Learn where you are. Learn about this place and its history. Learn not only the history of its people but the history of the land itself, its deep history. Learn to adapt your ideas and institutions to that land. Learn to work together if you mean to endure.

2

Water as a Tool of Empire

The dictionary on my desk defines water as "a clear, colorless, nearly odorless and tasteless liquid, H_2O, essential for most plant and animal life and the most widely used of all solvents." As definitions go, it is functional enough, for most readers, whatever their gender, class, or ethnicity, will be equipped to understand it. They will generally have their biological senses intact, will know a little about chemistry, and will have washed dishes at one time or another and watched the grease dissolve down the drain. They will also, however, have likely thought about water in far more complex ways than that little three-line definition could possibly capture, and to leave out those other thoughts is to strip water of virtually all its richer interest and meaning.

Water has had an incredibly complex cultural history. It has been as vital to our minds as to our bodies and has been among the most widely used of all metaphors as well as solvents. Although historians will not be surprised by such a claim, we have not yet written the cultural history of water for any of the major or minor cultures, ancient or modern. In thinking about the past, we tend not to think about water at all, or we unconsciously think about it in the cultural terms most familiar to us— that is, in the terms of modern civilization. Today water refers mainly to a commodity providing material comfort and prosperity. Modern people, including historians, think less about its mythic, allegorical, or religious past, its relation to life and death, to moral regeneration or salvation, and more about its many uses in the economy. We expect it to be as clear, colorless, and odorless as we can get it, and then we dismiss it from consciousness. With hardly any effort on our part, it comes gushing from a tap, while the means by which it has reached us are taken for granted. But this will no longer do in an era when water has become a global issue: a substance increasingly scarce, polluted, and fought over. It is time for historians to look more closely at this substance and the forms it has taken, the roles it has played, and to probe the meaning of water beyond what the dictionary provides.

During the nineteenth century, writes the historian Jean-Pierre Goubert, "water, which had once been a gift of God or of nature and a privilege reserved for the nobility, now became the property of everyone and subsequently went on to acquire the status of industrial product." He refers to this transition as the "conquest of water." Through miraculous new technology, water became an abundant, democratized resource. Water was made to turn the wheels of industry and earn enormous profits from making textiles. Water technology altered the landscape and waterscape, the shape of towns, the relation of city to country. People were not the same creatures they were before the conquest, for they had been changed as much as their environment. For one thing, people in advanced technological societies came to depend on having an abundance of water and to depend on those who furnished it. Moreover they expected to consume far more water than their ancestors did. In Paris, the European capital of the modern conquest of water and its purification, per capita demand went from about ten liters daily on the eve of the French Revolution to over two hundred liters by 1900. The conquest brought new emphasis on and new standards of cleanliness and health. To be civilized meant that people must take a bath every week and use a water closet instead of an outdoor privy. Beginning in the last century, the conquest of water became a central preoccupation, one of the main themes in the modern secular religion of progress.[1]

But my main subject is not this conquest of water for the sake of urban sanitation or industrial production, or the enhancement of city water supplies, or the gospel of cleanliness, as described by Pierre Goubert for France. Although I will later argue that the growth of the metropolis was a decisive force behind all aspects of the global conquest of water, I want to deal particularly with the conquest of water for agricultural purposes. By far most of the water consumed in the world today, 70 percent of the available freshwater supply in fact, goes for agricultural crops, not water closets. Approximately 270 million hectares of land are currently under irrigation. A large part of the world's population depends on those hectares to stay alive; one-third of the world's food is grown on irrigated lands. Irrigation was not pursued much in Europe, which has plenty of rainfall in most places (Spain and Italy are the chief exceptions), but it became common and essential in many parts of the world where the Europeans went to live and rule—in the exotic arid lands of Asia, Australia, Africa, and the Americas. The driving purpose of the Europeans was to win those lands over to their new religion of progress and make them support their new metropolitan standard of living. This agricultural conquest of water, like the urban conquest in France, depended on a profound change in thinking about water. It became less a sacred, purifying gift from God and more an instrument of secular materialism.

So extensive and monumental has this quest for agricultural water been that its impact on the biophysical world has become far more devastating than all the city water systems combined. It has flooded whole valleys, destroyed riparian ecosystems, turned dryland habitats into artificial oases, stimulated disease organisms as well as improved health, allowed the human population to grow to dangerously high levels, changed the life of estuaries, and perhaps changed the patterns of rainfall on the earth.

The leading symbol of this conquest of water is the large masonry or concrete dam, and arguably it is the leading icon of progress throughout the world today, from the fabled Indus and Yangtze rivers of Asia to Africa's Zambezi and Zaire rivers to the Colorado River and Rio Grande of the American Southwest. The dam represents the blessings of technology, economic development, and modernity. Though dams have been constructed throughout history, the earliest appearing in ancient Mesopotamia, it was during the nineteenth and twentieth centuries that they became key symbols of European wealth and power, indeed, along with the railroad, they became the most important artifacts of European imperialism.

By 1878 the European nations controlled 67 percent of the world's land surface; by 1914, 84 percent. The causes of that extraordinary expansion of power are multiple, involving both motives and means; the Europeans, for diverse reasons, wanted to dominate the earth and, at the same time the motive appeared, they acquired the technological means to do so. As Daniel Headrick has written, technological changes "made imperialism happen, both as they enabled motives to produce events, and as they enhanced the motives themselves." Among the most important of those technological changes were those going on in hydraulic engineering, including canals, headworks, and dams. To a large degree, European imperialism rested on the transfer of that hydraulic engineering and water-controlling apparatus to the rest of the world—spreading "the tools of empire," as Headrick has put it, with profound consequences both for the natural environment and the human community. This was a long-term consequence, for what the Europeans left behind, when they lost political control of all that territory, was a continuing fascination with machinery, innovation, and the conquest of nature. "This," writes Headrick, "has been the true legacy of imperialism."[2]

If the French became the leading architects of a new urban water regime, the British led the way toward modern irrigated agriculture. India was the first target of their conquest, and from that country a model of agricultural water development went out to Egypt, Australia, South Africa, and the American West—old and new societies alike, sharing a common condition of aridity and a common determination to overcome it. Long before their railway system was of any importance, the British had covered England and Scotland with canals for the purpose of transportation; they learned how to make water run in the directions that were most useful to them. Once in India, however, they discovered that the great need was not canals to carry barges but canals to bring water to the desert and extend cultivation. India already had a few such structures, notably those drawing water from the Jumna River in the north-central part of the country, which had been built centuries ago but had fallen into disrepair and in many places were covered with jungle. In 1830 the British engineers, mainly recruited from the Bengal artillery, tackled the rehabilitation of the Jumna canals. Six years later they began to make a massive new canal of their own on the Roorkee plateau between the Jumna and the Ganges rivers—the world-famous Ganges Canal, 10 feet deep, 170 feet wide, 900 miles long, designed to irrigate almost 600,000 hectares. The Ganges Canal opened in 1854 and proved to be a fabulous technical success. By the twentieth century, it was feeding two and a half million people and returning nearly 12 percent a year on the cost of its construction. Such irrigation works, the largest the world had ever seen, promised to alter poor, backward societies forever.

Following those successes the British water experts spread canals over the rest of India. The success of those canals depended, of course, on the level of Indian rivers, which in turn depended on the monsoon, the snowpack in the mountains, the summer runoff. Eventually engineers learned how to store water as well as draw it off, by building barrages and dams on the main river courses and near the headwaters. With such works they could irrigate lands such as the Sind and the Punjab, where agriculture was otherwise impossible, and the Gangetic plain and much of the Deccan, both vulnerable regions where sometimes the rainfall was adequate and sometimes not, causing frequent crop failures, famines, and social unrest. Irrigation projects became a means of pacifying a volatile country; control the water and thereby control the people, who in times of drought might grow hungry and mutiny against the empire. Even after they threw off their rulers, the Indians would not return to their old relation with water. Richard Baird Smith, one of the leading imperial engineers, was right when he predicted that the canals and dams were "more likely, from their relations to the material prosperity of the country, and from their permanent nature, to perpetuate the memory of English dominion in India than any others hitherto executed."[3]

I have been intrigued by the way in which this hydraulic model of progress and development passed from India halfway around the globe to the western part of the United States in the later decades of the nineteenth century, reversing the flow of ideas that Americans believe is natural and right. Americans learned to think about water in the same terms of conquest as the French and British. They, too, wanted to build canals and water-driven factories, city reservoirs and conduits, to enjoy the same material benefits the Europeans enjoyed. Instead of expanding overseas, however, they expanded westward across the continent and founded an empire of their own, linked by railways to their central cities. As it happened, much of that empire to the west was as arid as the one the British acquired in the southern hemisphere. Beyond the hundredth meridian of North America, as John Wesley Powell first pointed out in 1878, the average rainfall is below 20 inches a year, insufficient to support the major food crops. To conquer that land meant to conquer the water and make it serve the ends of national production.

The Mormons were the first Americans to undertake that conquest, beginning in the late 1840s. In their desert kingdom of what is now Utah isolated from contact with the broader currents of American and European imperialism, they proceeded naively, by a folk process of trial and error, to invent their own tools of water management. But that approach was not sufficient for Americans elsewhere in the West, who had grander material ambitions than the Mormons and a compelling religion of their own called "progress." They sought expert instead of folk experience, and they found it in British India. Beginning in the 1870s, western Americans, particularly engineers and scientists, began a pilgrimage to the Ganges Canal and its counterparts to discover exactly how the comprehensive conquest of water might be carried out. As one of those pilgrims, George Davidson of California, put it: "India affords us the most conspicuous examples of irrigation on a grand scale, and it is here more than anywhere else in the world that a great systematic scheme is in progress of development."[4]

Sometimes the connection among the practitioners of water conquests was more than a single fact-finding tour abroad or a book ordered from a foreign land. Sometimes it was an expert himself who migrated and took up work in another country, becoming a direct agent of technology transfer. For example the bible on hydraulic engineering in the late nineteenth-century United States was written by a Los Angeles engineer named Patrick Flynn; before coming to the United States in 1873, he had been an engineer in the Public Works Department in the Punjab, designing waterworks for internal colonization schemes there. We need to study more closely this international, mobile "priesthood" presiding over the creed of development through the conquest of water. Who were they and what was their training? Did they speak a common language despite their national differences? What did they conceive as the ends of their science and technique? What attitudes toward nature or water did they hold? What were the dominant metaphors they used in thinking about rivers, floods, or aridity? What kind of society did they think they were constructing along with the hydraulic system, and what did they really get?[5]

One conclusion the global engineering priesthood leaped to early on was the absolute necessity of centralized government planning, management, and ideally, ownership of water. The conquest demanded the state's commitment—its money, its authority, its bureaucratic oversight. In India the Jumna canal system had collapsed when an ancient government fell apart, leaving the water system unmaintained and undefended, and no one had ever been able to put it back together until the British arrived and made it a state project once more. Moreover modern private enterprise, though frequently urged to invest in new water projects, had generally failed to do so. It commonly took twenty years to begin making a profit from an irrigation investment, and no company could wait that long to get its money back; they went bankrupt first, or they sold out to the government. The private investors suffered too from what the Australian irrigation engineer Alfred Deakin called "the universal ambition of engineers to preside over massive and handsome masonry headworks," which drove up the costs of construction considerably.[6] After at least four major private failures, the colonial government took over completely the building of water projects in the subcontinent. George Davidson noted in 1874 that "all the principal works now in progress or that have been undertaken for the past ten years are in the hands of the government. Private enterprise, never heartily engaged in this kind of work, appears now to have been compelled to abandon the field."[7]

The lesson for the Americans in that experience was clear, if difficult to embrace. The only agency capable of planning and financing the full conquest of the arid West, they began to realize after a long period of their own piecemeal, underfunded local and private efforts, was the federal government in Washington. But the American government stood in a very different relation to its citizens than the British colonial government did to its lowly colonial subjects. Americans prided themselves on their self-reliance, their independence from outside authority, and they felt a vehement suspicion toward all government, dating back to their own eighteenth-century rebellion against the British imperialists. They were the first colonialists to win their freedom, and they cherished the memory of that struggle to the point of resisting ever after the expansion of federal power in the United States. Nonetheless, despite a lot of hesitation and grumbling, they did accept that expansion in the case of water development; indeed, they *demanded* it. Their religion of progress required it.

In 1902 Congress passed the National Reclamation Act, which put the federal government irrevocably in charge of almost all future irrigation development in the West. Though the government would never actually own the water, most of it already having been appropriated by private citizens except on the federal lands, it would henceforth dominate water development.

Even then it was more than three decades later before the U.S. government completed its first great monument to the conquest of water in the West, one worthy to compare with the achievements of British India. That monument was Hoover Dam, dedicated in 1935 (it was first called Boulder Dam), the first high dam in the modern world, rising out of the deep twisted canyons carved by the Colorado river to a height of over 220 meters and creating an immense reservoir, Lake Mead, of 37 million cubic meters capacity. Hoover Dam controlled dangerous floods, generated electricity, and stabilized an irrigation supply for California agribusiness. American engineers boasted that it was one of the greatest technological wonders of the age. The British and French experts may have been more skilled in precisely controlling the flow of water through ditches, but it was American experts who showed the other countries how to achieve the ultimate in brute, muscular force, pouring enough concrete to stop the mighty Colorado in its tracks and eventually controlling it from headwaters to mouth, spreading nearly every drop of its water on the land. Following the success of Hoover Dam, the U.S. government, through its construction agency, the Bureau of Reclamation, built nearly four hundred large storage dams throughout the West, until every major river had become a federal artifact.[8]

In developing the American West, the government soon discovered that it needed more than world-class engineering and centralized planning. The water so expertly commanded had to be used for agricultural production, and used efficiently, or the whole project of conquest was incomplete. The government needed agriculturists who understood the imperatives of progress, who had money of their own to invest in the project, and who thought in the same terms of resource efficiency. Government, in short, needed active partners on the land.

Where in the rural world could one find those partners ready and able to participate in the conquest? In India the British authorities had, by and large, only backward peasants to work with, a situation that proved their undoing time and again. Despite some splendid technical successes, the British experts floundered repeatedly when they tried to teach peasants how to be modern agriculturists; there simply were not enough men ready and able to match the technology. Such men needed to be part of the rising order of agricultural capitalists, not peasants, and have their eyes fixed on urban markets and the potential for profit, rather than on the village and its domestic needs. Only in the Punjab, where the government could carefully pick its partners from overcrowded districts and resettle them in colonies carved out of the desert, did much real, lasting success come. Elsewhere the recalcitrant Indian peasant was the persistent flaw in the grand design.

Critics dismissed the Indian farmer as a hopeless model for other, more progressive nations undertaking their own irrigation. "Squatted upon his hams, clad in a waistcloth, and often without vest or turban, the Hindu peasant bends above his irrigating channel," wrote Alfred Deakin, one of the peasant's most trenchant critics.

> He will stand up to his knees in water all day among his rice fields, and toil the whole twelve months through for a bare subsistence, but he will be very loth [sic] to try a new experiment, will never make a purchase, except on extremity, either of an improved seed or implement, and will cling to traditional ways so long as he can find the slightest pretext for justifying them. . . . A timid, industrious, inoffensive, domestic, gossiping hind, he exists mentally in as narrow a

plot as that upon which he works; his little horizon everywhere bounded by extravagant legend, absurd superstition and implacable fears. Living in abject poverty, material and intellectual, the little cunning he has acquired in dealing with his crops pertains solely to the state of nature in which he lives and works.[9]

Clearly in Deakin's mind the conquest would go along more smoothly if it could find better human material than an ancient peasant-based society provided. That was one of the most compelling lessons he learned from his extensive study of irrigated India, and he left the country to find more promising examples elsewhere, particularly in the American West.

The western part of the United States had a number of old, indigenous communities of peasant farmers too, Amerindians and Hispanos, not so different from those along the Ganges, but the whites decided to ignore them completely when they began constructing their dams and canals. Virtually none of the water would go to them. Where they were in the way of projects, using land or water the white newcomers wanted, they were removed and resettled elsewhere. "During the development period that has characterized western water affairs over the last one hundred years," write F. Lee Brown and Helen Ingram, the rural poor of the American Southwest "neither extensively benefited from, nor effectively participated in, decisions involving river compacts, dam or reclamation project construction, or most other major water events. In a number of important respects, developmental activities have actually been injurious to their interests."[10]

To be sure a few of the older, poorer ethnic communities survived in such backwaters of the modern West as northern New Mexico, places where even today water is viewed as a community resource to be held in common by everybody and managed by local people. In his book *Mayordomo*, Stanley Crawford has described in wonderful detail the life of one of those surviving traditional irrigating communities, located on the Rio de la Junta, which still holds fast to a relationship with water that is very different from the one pursued throughout most of the Anglo West. Their technology of control consists primarily of shovels and human muscle, coordinated by a loose consensus, the end of which is community survival rather than economic gain or bureaucratic power. "There are few other civic institutions left in this country," Crawford writes, "in which members have as much control over an important aspect of their lives; relatively autonomous, in theory democratic, the thousand *acequias* of New Mexico form a cultural web of almost microscopic strands and filaments that have held a culture and a landscape in place for hundreds of years." That web, however, has long been under pressure from outsiders who want to gain control of the water for their own ends, mainly economic growth in the urban-industrial centers of the state. Crawford fears that the surviving traditional Pueblo and Hispanic communities will someday lose out in court, as they have lost out in other parts of the world, and the water will flow to those with more money, influence, and lawyers. "Perhaps our logic," he continues, "has got turned upside down: in the north we should be saying that water is essential for keeping our communities together, and such is its main use now—as the substance around which a most remarkable tradition of self- governance adheres. To this, even agricultural use may be secondary."[11]

Crawford's point of view has not been common in the history of water development in the West. On the contrary the Americans tried to wipe the slate clean in ways that the British in India could not and to bring in a better stock of agriculturists: energetic, enterprising Anglo-Saxon settlers, who would lay the foundations for irrigation in the arid West. Alfred Deakin came to look them over and contrasted them favorably to the Old World peasants: "The alert, inquisitive, intelligent, restlessly inventive and progressive Americans," he wrote admiringly, a people who multiply "their machines and devices every year, bringing to their aid all the resources of scientific discovery, and to their management the keenest commercial spirit."[12]

To attract such people west, the U.S. government offered generous gifts of free land, stimulated railroad construction with land grants, and protected the interests of the favored white settlers from the older nonwhite inhabitants. As a result, when reclamation was federalized in 1902, it had available a group of new agriculturists in place, eager and ready for federal water projects to aid their enterprise, men who did not have to have it foisted on them but were clamoring for partnership. By the time Hoover Dam was completed, the federal government was almost exclusively devoted to providing cheap water to successful white settlers, many of them large agribusinessmen, not to landless or hungry or marginal people. Water development in the American West was primarily for those who had already developed themselves into men of property, efficiency, and productivity.

Here then in the twentieth-century American West, not nineteenth-century India, the conquest of water reached its highest all-round standard of economic achievement. The West could boast a talented cadre of scientists and engineers to design the technology and make it run efficiently. Despite many misgivings, it had entrusted itself to the hands of a strong central government that would invest vast public monies without worrying about a quick return or even about achieving a balance between costs and benefits. And it had attracted a class of progressive, entrepreneurial settlers, eager for more and more water; though intensely competitive in the marketplace, those settlers were prepared to work together long enough to get that water delivered to their ditches. Call the whole composite the holy trinity of modern water development—an alliance of Science, State, and Capital. By the time of World War II, they were a more or less stable, happy alliance, not agreed on every particular to be sure, but united by a common vision of turning every river of the West into personal wealth and national power. It was an alliance designed to achieve an empire over water unlike anything seen before.[13]

Around the year 1980, when I first began to look into the conquest of water in the American West, no historian had yet told the story of this evolving alliance of power. Many environmental battles had been fought over proposed dams and over the degradation of rivers throughout the West, and there was a substantial body of writing about those battles, but most of it was journalistic, and little of it touched deeper questions about the conquest and what it had cost in social as well as ecological terms. One of the best of those writings, John McPhee's widely read essay on the Colorado River, in which David Brower of the Sierra Club confronts Floyd Dominy of the Bureau of Reclamation, the most cocksure and most powerful of the water bureaucrats, had appeared in 1971, but even at that late date no western historian had yet glimpsed the cultural significance of dams or water.[14]

One of the first to begin remedying that neglect was Norris Hundley, who in 1975 published his pathbreaking study of the Colorado River Compact, an agreement crafted in the 1920s that divided up the river among competing users and opened the way to Hoover Dam. Hundley expressed a profound truth when he wrote that "control of the West's water means control of the West itself," but then he stopped short of answering the crucial question about who those controllers were or what they wanted to achieve by their control.[15] The major implication of the compact, he argued, was that control over the West shifted largely to the federal government, "the most powerful authority over the Colorado River and, by extension, over other interstate and navigable streams as well." "Today," he continued, "Congress possesses sufficient authority to virtually coerce the states to obey its commands." Perceptive words, but Hundley was not really a critic of that federal power, nor of the agency that effectively exercised it, the Bureau of Reclamation. He acknowledged that there were serious pollution problems caused by federal development and briefly mentioned that many others had questioned the entire cultural imperative to exploit rivers rather than preserve them, but Hundley did not include himself in that group of critics; on the contrary, he was by and large a supporter of the conquest. He belonged, along with so many others of his generation, to the old but still tenacious Progressive tradition in conservation and politics, which advocated a utilitarian view toward nature and called for even more centralized control over natural-resource development. The Colorado compact was, in his view, a step forward, because it overcame the fruitless squabbling among the southwestern states and local private interests over dividing up the river, allowing the federal government to bring the whole watershed, from mountain peaks to the Mexican border, under full control. If Hundley had any criticisms to offer, they were of the petty squabblers, whose narrow self-interest had for so long interfered with efficient river management.

That perspective, echoing the views of Theodore Roosevelt, Gifford Pinchot, and Frederick Newell, was the one dominating western water history when it began finally to take shape two decades ago. The subject was new, it made impressive claims to significance for the region's past, but its historians began with a familiar, conventional approach to understanding that subject, and more broadly, to analyzing the relationship of nature and technology to politics. That is still where the subject of water commonly remains today. Over the past two decades, a small group of water historians has gathered under Hundley's leadership, and they have written good books, but all tend to share Hundley's belief about the need to expand federal control (an expansion, they lament, that has too often been thwarted by conflicting private or state interests) and tend to share his view that western rivers are valuable primarily for their regional and national economic potential.[16]

On the positive side, those water historians of the West have brought to the forefront the important issue of how we are to interpret the course of events I have just summarized—the conquest of water that reaches from nineteenth-century France and India to twentieth-century America. But so far they have not, it seems to me, understood the larger issues adequately. On the whole they have been conventional and vacillating as interpreters. Norris Hundley's most recent book, *The Big Thirst*, a study of the history of water development in California, illustrates those qualities.[17] Although it has solidified Hundley's leadership of the group, receiving unanimous praise by them, and though it is indeed an impressive piece of scholarship and a readable narrative of events, the book has a few flaws in its general arguments. It presents a superficial interpretation of the impact of the conquest of water on the structure of power in the West, and by logical extension, anywhere else in the world.

Briefly, Hundley argues that the water history of modern California began with the gold rush of 1849, and since then the dominant pattern has been one of profit-seeking individuals grabbing as much water for themselves as possible, fending off effective government planning, distrusting engineers and other experts who might interfere with their freedom. In their pell-mell rush for water, they have monopolized, wasted, polluted, and overdrawn a scarce resource. Hundley blames this outcome on Thomas Jefferson, whom he identifies as the founding father of an American political culture that teaches extreme individualism, economic laissez-faire, and narrow-minded localism. Never mind for the moment that the gold-rush mentality that Hundley laments had little to do with the real Jefferson, a man whom we can hardly imagine promoting the unrestrained greed of the miners, and everything to do with the emergence of nineteenth-century capitalism. We can agree that Hundley is absolutely right when he argues that Americans have been "single-minded and aggressively self-seeking in their pursuit of wealth" as they have been in their pursuit of water, which in an arid land is a crucial means to wealth. What he does not see is how the pursuit and means of wealth have changed from early gold-rush days—how western Americans have come to depend on massive and complicated technology, on concentrated economic and political power, and on centralized planning to achieve wealth. He does not see the alliance of the holy trinity I have described, upon which so much wealth in the West today rests. He does not fully see the deeper, interlocking power of all those modern agencies engaged in environmental conquest.

In contrast to Hundley and the Progressive group of water historians, I have tried to describe the American West as a "hydraulic society," meaning a society essentially based on the large-scale technological manipulation of a severely limited supply of water.[18] The long-term trend in that society, I have argued, has been toward more and more concentration of power, allowing less and less real input from the citizenry, who, compared to their ancestors, have become fundamentally ignorant about the processes and costs of water control. Furthermore I have suggested that the *ends* of that control have not been examined critically either by those holding power or even by those without power, including farm workers and city folk, who only vaguely understand the world of water management and blindly ratify its achievements. Both groups accept without real questioning the cultural imperative of "growth" and "progress" that has worked to keep the conquest going and to shield it from much scrutiny.

I am aware that the conquest of water in the West is only part of a much more general conquest. My chief intellectual debts are to a brilliant group of philosophers, many of them European, who have probed far more deeply than historians of the West the relationship between modern technology and the social order: for example, C. S. Lewis, E. F. Schumacher, Jacques Ellul, Hannah Arendt, Martin Heidegger, Max Horkheimer, Ivan Illich, Rudolf Bahro, Karl Wittfogel, and Lewis Mumford. They have many differences of argument, but they all agree on the conclusion that the technological domination of nature, which has been the great project everywhere in modern times, leads not simply to freedom and democracy, as the conventional notion of progress teaches, but to the domination of some people over others. A genuine democracy, in which a true freedom for the individual and the community thrives, requires a different, less domineering attitude toward the natural world— a culture where greed and appetite are restrained by reason, virtue, and modesty (all of which, by the way, are great Jeffersonian values).

That the American West has pursued a policy of technological domination instead of accommodation toward nature is evident and agreed on by all. That it has not been unique in that pursuit is also obvious. The chief distinguishing feature of the West has been the fact that, unlike the rest of the United States, it has had to face an extreme scarcity of a vital resource and, in response, has carried water engineering to heights unseen elsewhere in the country or, for that matter, in the world. Thus the West has followed a familiar course, worked out by European imperialists and observable on many continents, and yet it has followed a unique course, creating a hydraulic empire of unprecedented scope.

Hundley himself demonstrates how far the West has gone toward developing a concentrated economic and political power in trying to satisfy its unlimited thirst. He points out that 85 percent of the water in California goes to agriculture, which means that a mere fraction of 1 percent of the state's population, the irrigating agriculturists, who are organized into a powerful set of rural institutions, control almost all of the water flowing out of the state's canals and pipes. The rest of the water has been seized by the largest metropolises, Los Angeles and San Francisco particularly, which have been motivated by what he calls an "urban imperialism." The Water and Power Department of Los Angeles, for instance, became "the most powerful municipal agency in the United States," Hundley writes, before being transformed into an even more powerful Metropolitan Water District, which controls water over the entire urban mosaic of southern California. These are only some of the leading players in the complex state water industry. Other agencies have shouldered into the picture as well. Hundley discusses the state's Department of Water Resources, which has accumulated in recent decades "unimaginable power," and the Bureau of Reclamation, "the mightiest federal agency in the West." The composite of all these institutions he labels, as I do, "the hydraulic society" or, alternatively, "the water establishment." But then after describing so accurately the structure of power (he leaves out of the alliance the scientists and engineers) and after acceding to so much of my own analysis, he abruptly turns around to deny that any structure really exists. The accumulated power suddenly dissolves before our eyes into what he calls "a war of fragmented authorities." Tellingly he does not describe any battlefield in that war. He asserts that a "war" for water is going on but does not show it. Where has such a deep conflict between all those supposedly "fragmented" water agencies really broken out? Where has it prevented a major water project in California or any other state over the past half century? In truth such a war does not exist, because the state's water establishment has worked assiduously to avoid serious conflict, and the only real challenge or resistance to their decisions has come from outsiders to the industry, mainly from a growing but still small group of environmentalists who resent the power of those who make decisions over the fate of rivers. The engine of water conquest is indeed a complex thing, with many different parts, and those parts indeed can grate against one another; nevertheless the engine has managed to work together well enough to reorganize every watershed in the West, turning all the great rivers into a flow of money.

My point is that the most powerful groups in the water industry may not have agreed on everything, but they have agreed on essentials. They share an instrumental view of nature and a materialist set of values. They have not encouraged internal dissent from those values, and they have not divided into implacably hostile ideological camps. So long as they have found more water to capture somewhere in the West, so long as they have not had to fight over a fixed or even diminishing supply, they have managed to cooperate effectively in the pursuit of power and wealth. They have achieved a highly stable division of labor: the federal government plans, finances, and builds the big projects, the engineers furnish the expertise, and the private entrepreneurs of agricultural and urban growth take most of the profit.

That this hydraulic establishment does not have any deeply considered vision, nor express a strong sense of justice, nor show any genuine concern for its environmental spillovers is all too true. But it is not irrational or chaotic when examined in its own terms, which are the terms of endless economic "development," or as a Bureau of Reclamation slogan once proclaimed, they are in pursuit of "total use for greater wealth." Apparently Hundley now finds those goals vague and inadequate, as I do, and proposes to put someone else in charge of redefining the public good. We need to set up a super water agency in the West, he insists, which will be "authorized to take charge." Such an institution would be staffed by the best minds available, and they would try to define a more coherent, enlightened set of goals and then manage the water accordingly.

What those goals might be, Hundley leaves unspecified, but the inspiration behind his reform proposal is perfectly clear. It comes out of that old Progressivism we have already alluded to—the "new nationalism" of Theodore Roosevelt and Herbert Croly. It is a nostrum pulled out of the mothballs and presented as the only *realistic, practical* strategy for the future.[19] It is based on the conventional view that progress has, on the whole, been a wonderful thing—it just has not gone far enough—and on the hope that, if the right people are put in charge, a more complete paradise will soon arrive. Such thinking was elitist when it was proposed by Herbert Croly back in 1909, and it is elitist now. It follows faithfully the logic of the advancing technological society, with its mania for efficiency, order, and instrumental rationality, merely pushing it one step farther toward rule by enlightened technocracy. It does not really question the whole project of conquering nature but only seeks to clean it up and spread the wealth a little more widely. Pragmatic in its language but utopian in its vision, Hundley's Progressivist approach to water in the West rests on an unwarranted optimism about the elimination of waste, the social control of technology, and the steering of progress; and like the "establishment" he criticizes, he and most of his fellow historians of water remain highly evasive about the ends of ecological domination. For more probing and realistic views, we need to heed the experience of other nations where the conquest of water has gone badly awry.

The water empire in the West came of age immediately after World War II, following a substantial increase in its funding during the New

Deal era. Now it was the Americans' turn to give to the rest of the world, India and all the other countries, a model to emulate: a vision of development in which water featured prominently and of the social forces needed to achieve it. In 1949 Harry S. Truman, taking the oath of office as president of the United States, announced that his country was now ready to move beyond its own borders to bring progress to anyone and everyone on earth. To be sure, at that point the American West was itself an unfinished project; most of the big dams were under construction or still on the drawing board. California had only a third of the population it has today, while overall the region's per capita income was below the national average. Nonetheless Truman was eager to move on to the next great challenge of developing the rest of the world.

> We must embark on a bold new program for making the benefits of our scientific advances and industrial progress available for the improvement and growth of underdeveloped areas. The old imperialism—exploitation for foreign profit—has no place in our plans. What we envisage is a program of development based on the concepts of democratic fair dealing.

Truman was specifically proposing his famous Point Four program that would extend technical and economic aid to the so-called "underdeveloped" countries in the southern hemisphere. Undoubtedly as a strong supporter of western water-control projects (the government had appropriated $230 million for reclamation work that same year), Truman had in mind the exporting of many, many Hoover dams to other countries. His commissioner of reclamation, Michael Straus, described water development "as a prerequisite of all development and elevation of living standards" and boasted that "the American concept of comprehensive river basin development . . . has seized the world imagination. Yellow, black, and white men of various religions in all manner of garb are seeking to emulate the American pattern of development."[20]

To my knowledge, Truman's inaugural address is the first time the word "underdeveloped" appears in public discussion, suggesting that there must be a single ideal way of life that all nations aspire to, an ideal defined, of course, by North Americans.[21] What is especially astonishing is the extent to which leaders in the southern hemisphere accepted that label as fair and descriptive of their status. They were indeed underdeveloped, many readily admitted, and nowhere more so than in the utilization of the rivers that flowed through the lands; but with help from the

United States and other "developed" countries, they would overcome their inferiority. They understood, furthermore, that they would have to overhaul nature and themselves in the bargain.

Every part of the globe beckoned with projects, but Africa above all seemed a land offering untapped possibilities for comprehensive planning and development. Prior to World War II, the European powers had done little to develop Africa's water resources, except in the lower Nile valley, where British engineers had tried to secure control over Egypt and the Sudan through harnessing the river. Here was one of the most arid continents of all, yet its great rivers flowed freely down from the highlands and past dense lowland populations, wasting water and energy in the sea. Estimates of Africa's total water resources vary from 3.5 to 4.6 billion cubic meters, a little less than half of that contained in rivers and lakes, the rest in underground aquifers. The Zaire basin alone annually provides 1.3 billion cubic meters of water, followed by the Niger, the Ogooue, the Zambezi, the Nile, the Orange, and other smaller rivers. At the time of Truman's inauguration, Africa could boast 30 percent of the world's hydroelectric potential, but virtually none of it had been exploited. Below the Sahara Desert, it was irrigating less than 1 percent of its cultivable land, and all of that by native, small-scale technologies. Great possibilities abounded then, and in the late fifties and early sixties, with the end of formal European colonialism, faced with explosive human fertility and growing urban demand, Africa's leaders began to seek the aid of the Americans, Russians, and Western Europeans, along with such international agencies as the World Bank and the Food and Agriculture Organization, to take command of the waters. They were as bedazzled by the vision of a high dam rising in their country as Americans in the arid West had been.

The High Aswan Dam of Egypt has been the most discussed project completed over the past four decades in Africa, but it has had plenty of companions on the roster of megatechnic marvels. The still uncompleted Jonglei Canal, designed to capture the Nile before it loses itself in the swamplands of the Sudan, is on that list, as is the Akosombo Dam, built in the sixties in Ghana under the presidency of Kwame Nkrumah, creating a lake that drowned five percent of his country. In southern Africa the Kariba Dam and the Cabora Bassa Dam, both on the Zambezi, have become powerful symbols of the conquest, and so is the grandiose Transaqua scheme, though still only a blueprint, to divert the Zaire River northward to water the Sahel and so is Colonel Quaddafi's dream of the Great Man-made River Project, which, at a cost of $25 billion, would pump fossil water from beneath the Sahara and send it north to irrigate the Libyan coast. Clearly, from the ambitious size of these projects, it would seem that Africa is more than ready to match the faith in technology shown in the American West.[22]

Yet beginning around 1970, unsuspected problems began to appear with every large-scale water engineering scheme in the world, and it was Africa that suffered some of the worst headaches of all. Building the Akosombo, for example, required the displacement and resettlement of the people living in 740 widely scattered farming villages, as well as trying to force them through an agricultural revolution. The Kariba, which was designed to provide electricity for copper mines in Zambia, inadvertently damaged fisheries, destroyed floodplain farming, and forced the evacuation of tens of thousands of small farmers.

Africa's elites subsequently made a few adjustments in their planning. After sacrificing so many of their village agriculturists to satisfy urban electricity needs, they tried to refocus their water-development plans on increasing agricultural production through irrigation. But that shift, which took place during the past two decades, did not avoid all the problems the earlier dams created; quite the contrary: the newer projects brought more nightmares than ever. Development costs for irrigation sometimes exceeded twenty thousand dollars per hectare, an outrageous expense on a continent where many farmers earned only a few hundred dollars per year. Downstream habitats and communities continued to suffer from losing their silt-bearing floodwater, a great source of fertility, now trapped behind dams built for the sake of upvalley irrigators. Peasant farmers continued to be shoved aside in favor of more enterprising men, much as they had been in the American West or India. Worse yet, the new wave of African irrigation projects did not really solve the basic needs of the countries. According to Cambridge geographer Kevin Kimmage, "large-scale irrigation projects have been widely perceived as having failed to either reduce food deficits or increase agricultural productivity in Africa." Consequently Jon Moris, a research officer with the Overseas Development Institute of London, has argued that "irrigation technologies represent bad investments for African development precisely because of their intensive, bureaucratically controlled, quasi-industrial character." And environmental journalist Fred Pearce reports that, following so much failure in the quest for water development, many African specialists are beginning to look wistfully backwards "to the days before Western ideas about technology and ownership of the natural environment took hold."[23]

But it is back to India, where modern irrigation began, that we must turn to find the most intense dissatisfaction with and the most thorough critique of the Western model of water development. What the British introduced has been faithfully carried on by the Indians themselves. Since gaining independence in 1949, India has built more than a thousand new dams, until today it has more such structures than any other country in the world. Altogether in the postindependence period, it has spent over 100 billion rupees on developing irrigation facilities; yet the return on that investment has been far less than anticipated. The grain yields have frequently not met planning goals. Immense projects have destroyed forests and wildlife, increased runoff, contributed to soil erosion, and dried up village wells that depend on underground replenishment. More than twenty thousand villages now have no local drinking water. At the same time, ironically, many areas have become waterlogged for lack of proper drainage of their irrigated fields, while others have been poisoned by salt deposits caused by improper irrigation. Silt washing from the deforested hillsides has collected behind dams, lowering their storage capacity; the Sriram Sagar Dam in Andhra Pradesh, completed in 1970, lost a third of its capacity in two years because of silt building up on the reservoir bottom. Water-development projects have displaced people as well as soil—as many as two million a year—and often they have been resettled, if at all, on smaller parcels of land that cannot be cultivated. Critics complain that this ongoing devastation of rural India is part of the imperial legacy the British left behind, though it is Indian officials and experts, following the guide of their old masters, who have committed so many recent blunders.

To bring the new imperialists to an accounting is the aim of a younger critical generation, many of whom are admirers of Mahatma Gandhi and his ideal of preserving peasant communities as the foundation of India rather than following Western metropolitan models. Prominent among them is Vandana Shiva, a physicist become environmentalist, who writes in one of her recent books: "The temples of India, dedicated to the river goddesses were substituted by dams, the temples of modern India, dedicated to capitalist farmers and industrialists, built and managed by engineers trained in patriarchal, western paradigms of water management."[24] What is it that critics like Shiva seek in a postimperial, anti-Western relationship with water? No more large dams, to begin with, either for hydropower or irrigation. The problem with such projects, they say, is that dams interfere massively and violently with the natural water cycle and inevitably degrade the environment. The engineers may know how to pour concrete and manufacture turbines well enough, but they do not understand fully how the complex world of nature works. Their knowledge is necessarily limited and flawed; their projects are an imposition on nature rather than an accommodation to it. Dams testify to the great egos of their promoters, but they have all the classic weaknesses of hubris.

Similarly, it is charged, large dam and irrigation projects have, from the nineteenth century on, been imposed on traditional rural communities by outsiders who have shown little respect toward the accumulated wisdom of traditional rural people. Such people have been seen as inefficient and unproductive in their relations with the natural hydrology, when in fact they may have been well adapted to the complexities of their environment. So, the argument of the new generation of critics goes, stop building large dams altogether. Allow rural communities the freedom to work out their own improvements in their own terms. Help them build small water projects to serve their local needs. Help them maintain their forests, their vital watersheds, and to store water where it is most wisely stored—in underground aquifers, where it does not evaporate under a blazing sun and where it can replenish the springs and wells that village life has long depended on. Above all, let the people define their own needs for water in harmony with their traditions. Let them devise their own means to meet those needs, with only modest, unobtrusive financial or technical aid from the urban centers.[25]

The weakness in that critique is not that it will not work for the rural people that critics like Shiva want to save; undoubtedly it is the only strategy that *will* save them. Rather the weakness is that the strategy is focused exclusively on preserving the old ways of life. However, the question preoccupying policymakers in most countries is how to meet the growing water demands of the nontraditional, nonrural part of society, the increasing numbers of urban and industrial consumers. How are they to slake their great thirst? How are they to be fed without drastically transforming the countryside, without adopting modern irrigation, without abandoning the old agriculture and bringing in large water projects?

The entire imperial tradition of water development has always had urban people, not the peasantry, in mind. In the past those urban people lived in such places as London or San Francisco; today more and more of them live in the Third World centers of Bombay or Mexico City. It was for them that the rural water economy, like the rural use of land, had to be revolutionized. We cannot exaggerate the profound power of this historical force. The conquest of water has been essentially a metropolitan project, designed for if not always by the people living in cities, whether it has been nineteenth-century Paris sucking water from its countryside or modern-day Accra draining food, water, and electricity from its Volta River projects. The holy trinity of water developers have all been thinking about the metropolis, whether as a place to sell irrigated crops or hydropower or simply the commodity of water itself.

By the end of this century, as the modern global culture of materialism continues to expand, the number of people living in metropolitan areas will total nearly two billion, or one-third of the world's total population. Africa will have 340 million living in its cities by the year 2000, and by the year 2025 it will have 900 million. India will have 750 million, then double that number.[26] The developed (or is it overdeveloped?) American West will show similar patterns of urban growth, continuing trends evident since settlement first began, but especially accelerating after World War II. No traditional heritage, no folk wisdom, no primitive technology of shadufs and bamboo pipes or of village acequias and artesian wells, no local community organization, no grass-roots democracy, can possibly capture enough water to satisfy, directly or indirectly, those booming metropolises and the consumer demands that have created them.

Here then is the difficult predicament that we are in today. The great conquest of water, which began in Europe and moved to the far corners of the earth, is beginning to lose its appeal as a clear, compelling cultural ideal. Everywhere the large dam and all of its appurtenances are under attack by urban and rural groups alike for being too wasteful, destructive, and megalomaniacal. Water imperialism is beginning at last to be discredited. Water development is an idea lying in moral ruins. Indeed the whole concept of development is in disarray, and no one knows what it means anymore, or for that matter knows what a condition of "underdeveloped" must be. We are, therefore, approaching the end of a long chapter in human history, the era of the unquestioned conquest of nature in the name of material progress. Yet the next chapter begins in deep uncertainty about its plot or outcome. The history of the past two centuries has left us in a trap that has no easy escape. Where will the water come from to support those urban masses of the present and the future? Will irrigation continue to use 70 percent of the available supply, and if it does not, how will the masses, a large portion of whom depend on irrigation, be fed?

The old promise of an endless abundance now seems a receding illusion. Scarcity is looming in every country, even the well-watered ones. Who will control this increasingly scarce resource on this densely populated planet? Will the old imperial elite—the holy trinity of water development, State, Science, and Capital—continue in power into the foreseeable future? Will they extend their authority and remain the ones making the critical decisions about this vital resource? Or will a new, less agriculturally oriented elite rise and take their place, a group of industrialists perhaps, claiming water for their own ends, or perhaps Norris Hundley's disinterested, technocratic elite, allocating the resource according to their own ambiguous standards of value? What will the cultural history of H_2O be in a future of such pressing demands? All tough, resistant questions, and there is no longer enough water to wash them away.

3

Other Peoples, Other Lives

"Once we were happy in our own country and we were seldom hungry, for then the two-leggeds and the four-leggeds lived together like relatives, and there was plenty for them and for us." That is how Black Elk, a Lakota of the Ogalala band, old and nearly blind, sitting in a one-room log cabin with weeds growing out of the dirt roof on the Pine Ridge reservation in 1930, remembered the Indian past. Then he recalled how the Wasichu, the white men, came and how "they have made little islands for us and other little islands for the four-leggeds, and always these islands are becoming smaller, for around them surges the gnawing flood of the Wasichu; and it is dirty with lies and greed." The pain in that memory came not merely from the dispossession the Lakota endured, their loss of land and livelihood to the invaders, but also from losing their companions, with whom they once shared the country. The companions he had in mind were not the Crows, the Mandans, or the Cheyenne of the northern plains; they were the many tribes of animals who had lived for so long with the Lakota. In Black Elk's view, the idea of people included the trees, who were the standing people; the birds, the flying people; the fish, the swimming people; along with all those creatures that walked the land, whether on four legs or two. They were linked together in an ecological league of nations, and they went down together in defeat—dying out, retreating into the earth, or confined to reservations.[1]

Today it may seem ironic that anyone who lived by hunting them thought thus about animals. Black Elk's Lakota had traditionally lived by killing animals for meat, hides, furs, ceremonial feathers, or porcupine quills as an almost daily routine. Was that any way to treat one's relatives?

55

Yet in their mind there was no contradiction or irony. Killing animals was for them neither a crime nor a sin; it was the only conceivable way to live. They had not yet arrived at abstract, legal ideas of human, let alone animal, "rights" that would prohibit or restrain any killing outside the Lakota family circle. Although lacking a theory of such rights, they responded sympathetically toward all living creatures. Targets for their bows and arrows, animals were nonetheless their neighbors and companions, full partners in their community; the Indian concept of community, like their definition of peoplehood, did not make invidious distinctions among the species.

The killing and exploiting of animals is something we still practice in the American West, even if most of us actually see little of it going on or do little of it ourselves. Modern westerners may have as many hides and skins in our wardrobes, as much meat in our diets, as hunting Indians once did, though all of it comes to us without the smell of blood. We find it hard, however, to share the old Indian notion of plant and animal peoplehood. We cannot quite imagine how it was possible that once upon a time a nation like the Lakota thought it was all right to kill other creatures and yet did so with an expression of gratitude, of kinship, to the victim. According to the logic of our civilization, one must either deny the peoplehood of plants, birds, fish, and quadrupeds or completely avoid taking their lives; and since the latter seems so impractical, we rigidly deny the idea of their peoplehood altogether. That is our way of reasoning, and any other appears to us as sophistry or savagery. Perhaps nothing so completely separates the modern American from the traditional Indian as this difference in human perceptions of and relationships with the plant and animal world.

The idea of the peoplehood of animals and plants is completely alien to the vast majority of professional historians as well, who follow without much questioning the moral logic of their society. Historians make all the common assumptions about the sharp line separating the human from the nonhuman and carry those assumptions into their stories. For the most part, they ignore animals, wild or domestic, altogether; the only people they recognize in their books are the two-leggeds.

Western historians are not quite so unmindful as the rest of the profession on this matter; the four-leggeds in particular have played so recent, so conspicuous, and so central a part in the region's story that historians could not get away with leaving them out of the picture completely. If they have paid a bit more attention, however, western historians have looked on animals in very different ways from Black Elk and his Lakota tribesmen. Animals are no more granted peoplehood by western historians, even by western Indian historians, than by the average man or woman in the supermarket or furrier's shop.

Consider, for example, the history of the fur trade, which everyone agrees was an important part of western development. Obviously you cannot tell that history without putting a few beavers into it, but apparently beavers, to have a place in white history, should never show any ability to reason or converse, or be seen enjoying their lives, or even be alive. Beavers can only appear as "fur." That, at least, is how beavers appear in most historical accounts; they are not individual actors, nor do they form communities or families, but exist merely as depersonalized objects of the "fur trade." They are items of commerce and profit, significant only when they are dead, stripped of their skins and ready to be turned into garments.

The first great work on the fur trade, and still one of the most widely admired and most comprehensive, was Hiram Martin Chittenden's *The American Fur Trade of the Far West*, published in 1902. Its text runs to almost a thousand pages, but the beaver gets only four pages out of the whole; the rest is about company rivalries, trading posts, liquor, Indians, and "notable incidents and characters." Chittenden mentions the beaver in a couple of chapters called "Fauna," but his principal theme is that animals are "mines of wealth" inviting "the industry of the trader and trapper." We learn more about how to bait a steel trap with castor than about how the beaver lived and died. We learn that the export of furs to Europe ran as high as two hundred thousand annually, and that the average individual animal fetched from $4 to $10 in the marketplace, but nothing about the average size of a mother's litter or length of nursing. We read that the animal was stupid compared to humans: "One has but to examine his work," Chittenden writes, "to see that he has comparatively little idea of the art [of tree felling] as a successful woodsman practices it," and he adds that, were it not for the fact that trees along rivers tend to lean over the water and fall into it when cut, the beaver would waste most of its labor. In those same chapters on western fauna, the wolf appears too, but in an even more critical light. He is "the most ignoble of inhabitants," writes the historian, personifying "cowardice, beggary, craftiness, deceit, mercilessness, and all the group of evil qualities that are comprised in the term *wolfishness*." Chittenden's animals are people to this extent: some of them, like the wolf, are capable of evil, but none is capable of virtue. Most other historians of the fur trade have had even less to say about the lives and habits of animals.[2]

Domesticated creatures like cattle and sheep have also been vital to the western experience, and we have hundreds of books and articles on the industries that raised those animals for slaughter. The animals themselves have seldom if ever appeared in that literature as anything resembling Black Elk's "four-legged people." The first great historian of the range industry, Ernest Staples Osgood, looked at cattle through the eyes of a narrowly calculating cattleman: How much beef was out there on the range, he asked, and how did one raise and get it to the stockyards at a profit? How did one build up "a great and lucrative enterprise" and lay "the economic foundations of more than one western common-wealth"? Another range historian, Paul Wellman, in his rollicking yarn *The Trampling Herd*, nearly loses the herd altogether in his enthusiasm for gamblers, gunmen, and range wars, though he does briefly draw our attention to the intense suffering the herds went through in the winter of 1886, when thousands of unacclimated, undernourished animals died from the cold. The shining exception to the general cowlessness of the range histories is J. Frank Dobie's book *The Longhorns*, which gives a full, appreciative account of that breed's instinct, habits, and psychology— an animal, Dobie writes, that refused to be "dumb driven cattle" but insisted on following "the law of the wild, the stark give-me-liberty-or-give-me-death law against tyranny," a behavior that got them labeled "outlaws" and replaced by more docile Herefords. Even Dobie has trouble maintaining any interest in cows that are not so wild or so much a maverick.[3]

For a long time the history of the fur trade or the range industry dealt exclusively with two-legged people of the male gender, with white skins and pronounced entrepreneurial drives. Western history has been largely a story of strong men mastering and defeating strong, dangerous animals—men armed with guns, whips, skinning knives, ropes, and bridles. In this era of multiculturalism and gender-consciousness, that old exclusiveness has begun to change so that we now have fur-trade histories that include Indians as central figures, that talk about the frequent intermarriage of Indians and whites, that are openly critical of the impact of the white market economy on Indian lives. We have put women back into the story of cattle herding and roping, as we have Mexicans and blacks. Despite adding a more diverse cast of human actors, however, the "new western history" has so far remained indifferent toward the four-leggeds and their interests. Western history is still, even in more progressive accounts, a history that moral philosophers would call anthropocentric. It carries along assumptions of peoplehood that originated far back in the

European, indeed Judeo-Christian, tradition, which too often made animals soulless, contemptible creatures beneath human notice.

Yet consider how impoverished the story of the West would be if we omitted the animals altogether: no grizzly bears, no cattle or horses, no salmon, no wolves, no pumas, no grasshoppers or gulls or roadrunners. One could more easily leave General Custer out of the story than *Bison bison*. The military deaths at Little Big Horn had a great deal of symbolic but not much strategic importance; however, the bison, alive or dead, was symbolically *and* strategically crucial to Indians and whites.

Try to think of a frontier Plains where there were no bison somewhere in the picture. You cannot because they have centrally defined that part and period of the West, as they have materially supported its development and characterized it for the world as much as or more than any human figures you can name. Other animals have been there too, walking along all the trails, wandering through all the mining camps, breeding and eating on all the farms and ranches and national parks, prowling the edges of western cities, snuffling, bellowing, howling, gnawing on our minds as on our cabin doors. A West without animals would be like a Brazil without rain forests, an Iceland without ice. If they were all totally expunged, who would want to go there or read its history?

You might think that it is the particular responsibility of environmental historians to bring animals more fully into the picture of the western past. Even environmental history, however, has not so far succeeded in doing that; it too has focused overwhelmingly on people, on their battles over conservation policies, their struggles to safeguard natural resources (defined as whatever in nature is useful to humans), their efforts to create cultural landscapes. Part of the reason for that slant is that few environmental historians, if any, really believe that animals are a kind of people any more than other historians do—believe, that is, that they speak a language expressing a reasonably complex kind of thinking or some sort of culture, a language that we have simply forgotten how to understand. Put another way, environmental historians are modern in their approach to nature and do not share the cosmology of the Plains Indians, where wise little chickadees might whisper in your ear while you slept, warning of impending battles or giving advice about the world.

Be assured that I am not going to call on you to reject modernity, to deny the extraordinary achievements of human civilization, or attempt a return to the Indian hunter's livelihood or cosmology. I am not going to insist that animals can speak rationally to us or have something resembling culture or deep personal wisdom to reveal. Nor am I going to call for a history that has no humans whatsoever in it, that exchanges misanthropy for anthropocentrism. What I will do is argue that the life of the American West has always included the presence of animals—the wild and the tame—and that an adequate history of this region must give more attention to their presence and to the uses we have made of them.

To write that more adequate history, we need to rethink our traditional understanding and treatment of the animal kingdom. Barry Lopez is, in my mind, the most advanced and provocative thinker we have on the subject of animals, wildlife in particular, and from his writing I draw inspiration to begin that rethinking. "To set aside our relationships with wild animals as inconsequential," he writes, "is to undermine our regard for the other sex, other cultures, other universes. . . . What is required. . . is to rise above prejudice to a position of respectful regard toward everything that is different from ourselves and not innately evil." That involves, first, developing more complete images of animals than we have had, images that may in some cases come from science but also from the humanities. Historians need to go to wherever the animals are and encounter them in the wild in order to get better acquainted with their nature. In the second place, historians must join in a move to change the relationships we have had with animals. We have become owners rather than companions, and the animals in turn have become degraded to a merely instrumental or utilitarian status. Lopez goes on: "If we are to locate animals again at the complicated ethical and conceptual level of our ancestors, . . . we must decide what obligations and courtesies we will be bound by. The hunting contracts of our ancestors are no longer appropriate, just as their insight into natural history is no longer superior to our own at every point. These are to be new contracts."[4]

What those new contracts between humans and animals will be is still undetermined and must be the responsibility of all disciplines, all human beings. The special contribution of the historian toward that reformed way of thinking is to reveal what the relationship between humans and animals has been over time, how it changed in places like the American West with the coming of the Europeans, and what those invaders have learned or not learned through their experience. Such is the purpose behind the overview of western wildlife that follows.

The first white Americans to encounter the incredible array of animal life in the West were Meriwether Lewis, William Clark, and their party called the Corps of Discovery. They traveled mainly in the river valleys—the Missouri, the Snake, the Columbia—and hence saw only a portion of the fauna that dwelt in the region at the turn of the nineteenth century. Even so the list of species they added to science was extraordinary. In Paul Cutright's list of animals discovered by Lewis and Clark, I find such creatures as the channel catfish, the cutthroat trout, the soft-shelled turtle, the prairie rattler, the plains horned toad, the western grebe, the ring-necked duck, the piñon jay, Clark's nutcracker, the black-billed magpie, the broad-tailed hummingbird, the western meadowlark, the kit fox, the pronghorn, Roosevelt's elk, and the mule deer, the last of which they found roaming as far east as the junction of the Niobrara and Missouri rivers. "It is obviously impossible," writes Cutright, "for any person now alive to comprehend the abundance of game that once populated the plains of the West. Only on the African veldt in the pioneering days of Speke, Grant, Harris, and Cumming has there been anything comparable since man began recording history." Many of the animals had so little fear of humans that only a club could make them move out of the way. The novelty and abundance of the animals the explorers saw kept their spirits up, encouraged them to continue advancing despite the pain of towing and poling heavy boats upstream day after day.[5]

They did more than see; they also raised their muzzleloaders and shot at animals of every species they saw, killing them in large numbers on both banks, all the way from Saint Louis to Fort Clatsop. Mostly they killed for food. For nearly a month in their early days on the Missouri, they saw no Indians at all and had to depend on the meat they could hunt down. So it went for almost all the early explorers; they had to live off the land, which meant by and large they had to live on wild game. During a three-week period in May, 1805, as they moved through present-day Montana, coming closer to their first glimpse of the Rocky Mountains, Lewis and Clark recorded the shooting of 167 animals—that is, nearly 8 animals per day. On one typical day they took 2 deer, 3 bison, and 4 plover; on another they took 6 deer, 2 elk, and 1 bison. They saw their first bighorn sheep at the mouth of the Yellowstone River and thereafter shot them regularly, while watching more bounding among the riverine bluffs and cliffs. All that flesh fed a party of more than forty hungry men and one woman, plus outfitting them in leggings and furnishing elkhide ropes for pulling the boats. Remember that they were gone for twenty-eight months, and we can estimate that the number of animals shot to supply their daily needs must have amounted to something between five and ten thousand. Yet early on in the expedition, Lewis wrote: "Altho' game is very abundant and gentle, we only kill as much as is necessary for food."[6]

In fact they killed far more than they ate, and much of the killing had little to do with survival. It was done in the name of science, or it was done out of idle curiosity or for amusing sport, or it was an impulsive, vague gesture toward pacifying the wild. Clark was the first American to kill a pronghorn (he called it "a Buck Goat") and a coyote (which he described as "a Prarie Wollf, about the Size of a gray fox bushey tail head & ears like a Wolf, Some Fur[;] Burrows in the ground and barks like a Small Dog"), while Lewis has the distinction of being the first American to kill a grizzly bear, a male weighing three hundred pounds. Thereafter they shot at the big bears every time they saw them, and shot again and again, for it took as many as ten lead balls to bring one down. They killed mountain lions, snakes, gray wolves, bobcats, marmots, badgers, foxes, and undoubtedly hundreds of thousands of mosquitoes. On one occasion they poured water down a prairie dog's hole to see how much it would take to drown it. Theirs was, to be sure, no Ahab-like violence visited on the natural world for the sake of domination, no fierce implacable hatred against the wild lodged in a puritanical heart; theirs was a more banal kind of violence, practiced by men with such an abundance of ammunition and ease of opportunity that they regularly overcame their sense of restraint. On 29 May 1805, they came upon an immense pile of bison carcasses killed by Indians in a stampede over a precipice; "in this manner," wrote Lewis, "the Indians of the Missouri distroy [sic] vast herds of buffaloe at a stroke." Wolves were busy cleaning up the carrion, and they were so focused on their feasting that Clark could casually kill one with his espontoon. He would never have done that to any Indian on the scene; he was not that kind of man. But the wolf was in Clark's mind not another being like himself, to be tolerated and respected.[7]

Lewis and Clark came west at a time when European and American attitudes toward animals were beginning to change under the influence of the antislavery movement and democratic revolutions. What had been the conventional view, that animals fell outside the sphere of moral concern, was no longer so obvious. Within a few decades of Thomas Jefferson's ringing declaration, "All men are endowed by the Creator with certain inalienable rights," a few minds were wondering aloud why we should limit rights to men only. For reasons that are not yet clear, that challenge first came out of England, not the United States or France. Perhaps it had something to do with the strength of evangelical religion there, or with the popularity of sentimental fiction, or with the fact that England had long been a nation of pet keepers. In any case prominent writers and intellectuals took up the question and kept it before the public for decades to come.

The English economist and utilitarian philosopher, Jeremy Bentham, was foremost among them. He argued that, following the emancipation of African slaves, animals would have their turn at freedom and protection from cruelty, and he could see no reason why they should be put outside the protective circle of rights. "The question," he wrote in the 1780s, "is not, Can they *reason?* nor, Can they *talk?* but, Can they *Suffer?*"[8] Two decades later, in 1809, and just three years after the Corps of Discovery's return to the settlements, a Scottish politician introduced a bill in Parliament to prevent malicious and wanton cruelty to horses, oxen, sheep, and pigs. England, having only a few wild creatures left, a biologically depauperate country compared to the Great Plains of North America, centered its rights-of-animals debate on domesticated creatures—pets, livestock, creatures harnessed to drays and plows. They argued, with considerable passion, even violence, over whether it was permissible to beat horses that would not move fast enough or bait bulls before butchering them or pit cocks against one another to fight to the death. In 1824 a company of humanitarians met in Old Slaughter's Coffee House, London, to form the Royal Society for the Prevention of Cruelty to Animals. They were full of moral inconsistencies, to be sure, some condemning fox hunting while enjoying their fur mittens or pâté de foie gras, but what they had begun as a movement to bring about a new relationship with animals would spread far and wide, until it affected wild creatures as well as tame, and until it spread beyond London to the remotest corners of the English-speaking world.[9]

An American branch of the SPCA did not appear until 1866, led by the New York lawyer Henry Bergh. Long before that time, however, people going west had to wrestle with their conscience over the killing of animals. Lieutenant Zebulon Pike, for example, out to spy on Santa Fe in 1806–7, forbade his party to shoot freely at the abundant game they encountered along the way, in what is now Kansas and Colorado, "not merely because of the scarcity of ammunition, but, as I conceived, the laws of morality forbid it also." Apparently in his mind it was not wrong to invade a foreign country for the sake of espionage, but it was wrong to kill animals for the sake of amusement. Later, in 1840, the merchant Josiah Gregg, coming down the Santa Fe Trail one last time, brought along a few such humanitarian sensibilities of his own. Although by then the bison were becoming rather scarce, he and his fellow travelers found them in abundance along the Canadian River, leading him to observe that

> the slaughter of these animals is frequently carried to an excess, which shows the depravity of the human heart in very bold relief. Such is the excitement that generally prevails at the sight of these fat denizens of the prairies that very few hunters appear able to refrain from shooting as long as the game remains within reach of their rifles; nor can they ever permit a fair shot to escape them. Whether the mere pleasure of taking life is the incentive of these excesses I will not pretend to decide; but one thing is very certain, that the buffalo killed yearly on these prairies far exceeds the wants of the traveler or what might be looked upon as the exigencies of rational sport.

Honest man that he was, Gregg then admitted that the sight of the herds raised his own killing passions, and "I have not always been able wholly to withstand the cruel temptation." Seeing the bison grazing in such numbers, he piled off his horse, rifle in hand, and began to empty his chambers at the unsuspecting animals, killing three of them and likely doing what all his associates did—bringing back to camp their tongues as testimonials to his own manhood, his own "depravity."[10]

The consequence of such unleashed passions was a growing scarcity of animals. By the 1870s hunters were complaining up and down the Plains and farther west that the game had nearly gone, that they had to work harder and harder to find something to shoot. Among the most vociferous of those critics was Colonel Richard Irving Dodge, a military man and an enthusiastic hunter. In the spring of 1871, he drove a wagon past a single bison herd twenty-five miles long that had congregated in the valley of the Arkansas River. At least in that place, he recalled, "there was apparently no limit to the numbers of buffalo." Indeed they were so numerous that his "pleasure was actually marred by their numbers, as they interfered with our pursuit of other game." A year and a half later, the situation had changed considerably: "Where there were myriads of buffalo . . . there were now myriads of carcasses. The air was foul with sickening stench, and the vast plain . . . was a dead, solitary, putrid desert." He counted 112 dead bison inside a semicircle of two hundred yards radius, all killed by one man in less than an hour. Dodge estimated that in the years 1872–74, hunters killed over 4 million bison on the central Plains.[11]

In the colonel's view, such killing was excessive, and such excess was to be expected from the degraded humans who had come into the country to live following the defeat of the Indians and their removal to reservations. "Within the last few years," he wrote, "hundreds of men, too lazy or shiftless to make a living in civilization, have found a congenial mode of life on the plains. In season or out of season they kill everything that comes in their way." These were, in a manner of speaking, professional hunters. They set up a tent or hut out in the wilderness and began collecting hides and skins, selling them for as little as a dime apiece. They spent their earnings on flour, bacon, and beans— and on gambling and drinking—before returning to the wilds. "These men think only of today," Dodge protested. There were as yet no game laws to restrain them, and had there been, an army could not have enforced them. Their impact, Dodge feared, would be to drive all the larger animals to extinction in a few years, depriving sportsmen like himself of pleasure. Immediately following that critique, Dodge proudly added the record of one of his own hunts on the small tributaries of the Cimarron River: In twenty days he and four companions (another American officer and three English gentlemen, all men of the better sort) bagged 1,262 large and small animals. They counted among the fallen bodies 127 bison, 154 turkeys, 223 teal, 187 quail, a few antelope and deer, ducks galore, herons and cranes, hawks and owls, badgers, raccoons, doves, robins, and one bluebird for a "sweetheart's hat." A year later these same sportsmen came back to collect an equally diverse bag of 1,141 animals. Whatever bright flashes of life the depraved hide hunters had not shot for drink, these genteel and well-bred fellows took for their own more elevated enjoyment.[12]

No wonder then that, assaulted by both high and low levels of the social order, by loutish men who recognized neither law nor ethics and by civilized gents who wanted laws and ethics applied to everyone but themselves, the wildlife numbers of the West plummeted. As they did so, the country lost considerable charm and appeal. Stephen Long had once passed along the South Platte, noting how the profusion of wildlife enlivened "the uniformity of its cheerless scenery." John James Audubon had enthusiastically observed "an immensity of Game of all description" near Fort Union on the upper Missouri. John C. Frémont had written about the Platte Valley that, "in the sight of such a mass of life, the traveler feels a strange emotion of grandeur." Now blank uniformity was often all there was, the abundance had become rarity, and much of the grandeur had gone out of the landscape. The same eventually could be said for a large part of the West all the way to the waters of the Pacific, where sea otters, whales, and salmon declined in numbers as precipitously as the animals of the Plains.[13]

How many animals had there been in the West before Lewis and Clark, Pike and Long, Audubon, Frémont, Colonel Dodge, and all the dime-a-skin hunters arrived? For a long time, during more than a century of killing, no one had formed more than a rough impression of the wildlife abundance. The estimates ran to sweeping adjectives like "boundless," "innumerable," "infinite," and most helpful of all, "large." The first systematic effort to arrive at pre-Lewis and Clark faunal populations was made by the Canadian-born nature writer Ernest Thompson Seton in 1929. Seton had gotten something of a controversial reputation for his turn-of-the-century stories of animals that sacrificed their own lives to save others, of animals that "learned how" and "reasoned why," with little-children names like Johnny and Molly and Bingo. In those stories of individualized and highly humanized animals, he had tried to demonstrate, as he put it, "our kinship with the animals by showing that in them we can find the virtues most admired in Man," virtues like dignity, obedience, fidelity, and love.

> Man has nothing that the animals have not at least a vestige of, the animals have nothing that man does not in some degree share. Since, then, the animals are creatures with wants and feelings differing in degree only from our own, they surely have their rights. This fact, now beginning to be recognized by the Caucasian world, was first proclaimed by Moses and was emphasized by the Buddhist over two thousand years ago.

The point of his stories, he explained, was "to stop the stupid and brutal work of destruction by an appeal—not to reason, that has failed hitherto—but to sympathy, and especially the sympathies of the coming generation." By the late 1920s, however, the numbers of wild animals had fallen to their nadir, and Seton switched from telling heart-tugging, tragic stories of dying wolves and kindly rams to the greater collective tragedy of an entire continental fauna nearly wiped out.[14]

Seton's method was to glean from every published source he could find early and late estimates of the major game animals, to discover the extent of their original range, and to calculate how many animals per square mile that range might once have supported. Take the grizzly, for example, an animal found exclusively in the West, from the Great Plains to California and north to Alaska; no carnivorous species—indeed no species of any sort—so fully symbolizes the entire western region in its wilder days as this one. "In ancient times," Seton writes, "it was common to see a dozen of these monsters in a day's march." That was only an average experience, however; one northern California report claimed thirty to forty sightings in a single day, while another from the Big Horn Mountains of Wyoming claimed nine sightings over a month's span in 1877, and during salmon runs in Idaho, individual bears could appear along the creeks every 50 yards. By 1922, Seton calculated, there were only eight hundred of them left, all in Colorado, Wyoming, and Montana, the largest concentration being in Yellowstone National Park. Wolves had been far more widely distributed than grizzlies and were not a uniquely western animal. Seton estimated their original range as 7 million square miles, the widest of any large animal, and their original population he conservatively put at 2 million. By 1908 they had declined to 200,000, most of them dwelling remotely in Alaska and Canada, not in what had been their most favorable habitat, where they were now nearly extinct.[15]

Other animals, lower on the food chain, had been far more numerous than these predators before the white invasion. Seton calculated 60 million beaver, spread over a territory from the eastern United States and Canada south to the Rio Grande, excluding only the basin-and-range province of Nevada and the California deserts. There had been 5 billion prairie dogs, he thought, 800 million in Texas alone. Elk, or wapiti, had once roamed from Elk County, Pennsylvania, to the Elk Hills of California, amassing a continentwide population of 10 million. The more distinctly western herbivores, such as pronghorn, bighorn sheep, and mule deer had numbered from 30 to 40 million, from 1.5 to 2 million, and around 10 million, respectively. A government census in 1908 found only 17,000 pronghorn left in the United States, a nearly invisible fraction (5/10,000 of a percent, to be exact) of what they had been. Seton came up with a remnant sheep population of 28,000 outside of Alaska (based on 1922 data) and about 70,000 elk (in 1919), the largest number of the latter being in Yellowstone and none whatever on the Plains, where they had once lived in plenitude. Among the larger animals, the mule deer had survived best; there were still an estimated 500,000 of them at the time he wrote.[16]

Bison received Seton's most careful attention. They were, like the elk and wolf, not unique to the West but spread over an area of 3 million square miles, extending nearly to the East Coast. Using contemporary figures on cattle, horse, and sheep stocking rates on the old bison range, and allowing for differences between plains, prairie, and forest carrying capacity, Seton came up with a "primitive" population of 75 million of these animals, the most impressive large-animal population besides humans found anywhere on earth. By 1895, he went on, the number had fallen to 800, almost all of them within Yellowstone's borders, huddling against the prospect of utter extermination. In the next year the United States government finally passed its first law protecting the animal (President Ulysses Grant had pocket vetoed a protective bill twenty years earlier), and then it did so only because of a blatant poacher caught in the very act of killing and skinning those last bison in the park.[17]

Of course such estimates of original faunal populations are open to the charge of personal bias. Seton was dismayed at the destruction that had gone on, and he may be suspected of having calculated too liberally to heighten the tragedy. It is interesting to compare his faunal estimates with contemporary estimates of the pre-Columbian Indian population. The anthropologist Alfred Kroeber suggested in 1939 that the aboriginal human population had been 900,000 in North America and 8,400,000 throughout the hemisphere. Since that suggestion, other scholars have edged the standard estimates up and up, until in 1966 Henry Dobyns blew all previous numbers away with sensationally high estimates of 9,800,000-12,250,000 in North America and approximately 100 million in the western hemisphere. Dobyns's figures, more than ten times higher than Kroeber's, were supposedly based on better evidence about how many natives died from diseases introduced by the Europeans, dying before anyone got around to counting them. Here again there may be a hidden political agenda behind the revisionist campaign—a desire to make the white conquest appear far worse than we have ever acknowledged—but almost all scholars of the subject, including the most careful and objective, now agree that Kroeber's figures were too small.[18] In contrast to this lively debate, the project of determining historical faunal numbers has not gotten much farther forward than Seton left it in 1929. Did he, like Kroeber, underestimate the original animal populations, or did he embellish them? We simply do not know for sure. We cannot say how many wolves or widgeons or Mexican bats there were in 1492 or in 1805. We cannot, therefore, say with any precision what the full impact of whites has been on the fauna and ecosystems of North America or the American West.

The animal that has gotten the most attention from population revisionists is, predictably, the bison. Biologists think they understand this species better than Seton did, and they criticize some of his assumptions. He assumed, for example, a homogeneous habitat over the broad landscapes of plains, prairies, and forest, whereas a modern scientist would try to take into account the great local variety in those landscapes, including topographic gradients and the presence of wetlands that must have had some effect on the amount of forage available. Seton assumed that the bison were not nomadic, that they stayed within a year-round radius of one to four hundred miles; however, some experts since have believed that the animals migrated over much longer distances before the Union Pacific Railroad cut them into two separate herds and that, consequently, their numbers could not have been so large—vast areas must have been nearly empty of the species at times. Then too, Seton, though acknowledging the presence of predators and other competing herbivores, made only rough guesses as to what their impact might have been on the bison population. Finally some modern-day biologists wonder whether one can determine wild-animal food needs by looking at domesticated livestock and extrapolate reliably from cattle-stocking levels back to wild-bison numbers.

In the most comprehensive, detailed analysis yet offered, Frank Gilbert Roe estimates that only 40 million bison roamed the continent as late as 1830. And according to Dan Flores, "the Southern Plains might have supported an average of about 8.2 million bison, the entire Great Plains perhaps 28-30 million."[19] If we apply that sort of revisionist analysis to all of Seton's faunal estimates, they might diminish, too.

The bison dwelt mainly on the eastern side of the Rocky Mountains, with small, scattered herds wandering over the Great Basin of Nevada, Utah, and Idaho.[20] What was the original wildlife picture west of the plains? Biotically this country was comparatively meager in populations but diverse in species, the most diverse on the continent, due to its many mountain chains, forests, deserts, and grasslands. For this "farther West" (the eleven westernmost states, leaving out much of the Great Plains), a leading wildlife biologist, Frederic Wagner, has postulated an aggregated population of 20 to 30 million large mammals at the time of Columbus. He gives the following species estimates: bison, 5-10 million; pronghorn, 10-15 million; bighorn sheep, 1-2 million; mule and blacktail deer, 5 million; elk, 2 million. Note that he says nothing about predators, amphibians, mollusks, insects, or birds—only about the species that qualify as "game." Nonetheless those figures will do to give an idea of the landscape that Lewis and Clark passed through from Montana to Oregon, and of the size of the slaughter that occurred in that area, too.

One stark conclusion seems inescapable: When one considers the variety of species that became targets for hunters, all those species that Colonel Dodge boasted of bagging (included the bluebird for his sweetheart's hat) and more, the total animal death toll in the West was staggering. Barry Lopez concludes about the Plains in particular: "If you count the buffalo for hides and the antelope for backstraps and the passenger pigeons for target practice and the Indian ponies ([killed] by whites, to keep the Indian poor), it is conceivable that 500 million creatures died."[21] Five hundred million—a veritable holocaust.

The American West began to emerge as a region in the years following the Civil War, when the nation turned from fratricide on the eastern battlefields to devote its energies to peace and national economic development. That at least was the official story. In truth, men came west with plenty of guns in their hands still, sometimes the very guns they had used in battle; and perhaps hardened by all the bloodshed they had seen, they proceeded to shoot their way to a new conquest. Many of the westward-moving pioneers regarded the native human beings, standing in their way, as subhuman and had no qualms about shooting as many as they could. Generally, however, the invaders, like Lewis and Clark, drew an important line of difference when it came to killing. They acknowledged that Indians were people, if only an inferior kind of people, so backward that it was impossible to integrate them into civilized society. They sought to avoid killing them if possible and to use peaceful, legal means like treaties and court decisions to dispossess them—means that would take away their land but not their lives. It was, however, all right to wipe out completely the Indians' basis of subsistence and their companions, four-leggeds like the bison.

If we say that the white invaders followed a policy of "genocide," what we must mean is that the Indians were supposed to disappear peacefully, nonviolently, abstractly, cleanly. The animal nations of the West, in contrast, faced a different fate. They too were in the way of a great unifying project that would bring Northerners and Southerners together once more to create "the Great West," the last major region of opportunity and challenge on the continent. Here in the years after the Civil War was where the last large game animals dwelt. Here was a distinctive fauna, with many species and subspecies unrepresented elsewhere in North America, organized into a myriad of ecosystems: populous tribes and nations of birds, mammals, and all the rest, interacting in complex communities with each other. In contrast to the treatment of the Indians, it became a deliberate cultural imperative, even one pursued and funded by the federal government in the case of the bison and the predators, simply to eliminate those wild nations outright—the bison because they were the Indians' food supply, the predators because they threatened the whites' livestock. The wild animals could not sign treaties or go to court or accept bribes or get hooked on alcohol; they could not be brought, that is, by whatever nefarious or degrading means to acquiesce in their own dispossession. They must be gotten rid of by the gun.[22]

The West was to be the last and best version of the American dream, deriving wealth and civilization out of the wild landscape, but the dream opened upon a landscape littered with skulls and bones, drenched in blood. By far most of those bones belonged to the creatures that Black Elk called the four-legged people. More blood by far flowed from them than flowed at Antietam, indeed flowed throughout the entire Civil War. More living organisms died in that war on the frontier to create the dream of the West than in all the wars that America has ever fought.

Throughout the holocaust the Indians watched as their food, their companions, disappeared before their eyes. In some cases they participated in the slaughter, selling furs and hides in the market to get some of the whites' goods—guns, alcohol, sugar, and cloth. In other cases they watched in despair and bewilderment. Plenty Coups, a leader of the Crows in Montana, was among those trying to understand the vast faunal change taking place in the West and its implications for his people. At the age of ten, he had a dream of a coming day when the white men would take control of the country and put their cattle (their "spotted buffalo") to graze where the wild animals had once roamed. By his middle years, that dream had come true; the bison were gone and so was his people's way of life. "When the buffalo went away," he said, "we became a changed people. . . . The buffalo was everything to us." He refused to talk about his life after the passing of the great herds, for in a sense he had died then. "When the buffalo went away the hearts of my people fell to the ground, and they could not lift them up again. After this nothing happened." His interrogator, Frank Linderman, added to that sense of an ending a fuller explanation:

> Pitched so suddenly from plenty into poverty, the Indian lost his poise and could not believe the truth. He was dazed, and yet so deep was his faith in the unfailing bounty of his native land that even when its strange emptiness began to mock him he believed in the return of the buffalo to the plains, until white men began to settle there, their wire fences shutting off his ancestral water-holes. Then a bitterness tempered by his fatalism found a place in the Indian's heart. . . . His pride was broken. He felt himself an outcast, a pariah, in his own country.[23]

Eventually it became clear that the bison and all the other four-leggeds, along with so many of the people with wings and the people who crawled on the ground, had not merely "gone away." They were not in hiding, waiting for an opportunity to return. They were dead. A human way of life was also dead. And consequently for some observers, time itself had ceased.

Because of the magnitude and ferocity of the slaughter, many observers believed that virtually all the animals of the West must eventually disappear. Like the Indians, they must vanish before the charging engines of progress, which could neither slow down nor stop. That sense of inevitability was especially strong in the late nineteenth and early twentieth centuries, when populations dropped so precipitously and when hardly a state or territory, let alone the federal government, seemed willing to arrest their decline. By the 1920s, as Seton demonstrated, the West had reached the lowest point in its work of annihilation. In a sense that decade was the real end of the frontier era, not Frederick Jackson Turner's 1890s. When all the wildness had been expunged from the country, and no more wolves were left to send shivers down the spine, then the West was truly won.

But then, surprisingly, many of the animals, like the Indians, did not vanish from the scene. They began a comeback from the edge of extinction, aided in some cases by two-legged people devoted to a new ideal of wildlife conservation. Those people wanted to save not all the species that were endangered but those in which humans had a strong interest; and the strongest interest of all was that of the sportsman seeking prey. Save wildlife then as recreational opportunity for the sportsman. Save the outdoor life of the hunter, which since Lewis and Clark had been a part of the frontier experience. Save the Old West by saving its "game." Such was the plea that began sounding as early as the 1870s, until a half century later it had produced an organized national crusade, backed by money, expertise, and social status, all devoted to rescuing the major game animals from a certain doom. The conservationists succeeded in their crusade to a wonderful degree, and they did so by enlisting the agency of the federal government on their behalf—turning to modern bureaucracy, ironically, not to preserve nature of and for itself but to preserve a tradition of strong, self-reliant men going out into nature for rugged adventure.

For a long time the contributions of sport hunters and fishermen went unappreciated by historians, who tended to focus on such figures as John Muir and Gifford Pinchot as the founders of American conservation. The first general history of wildlife conservation did not appear until 1975, and it was written not by a historian but by a professional wildlife specialist, James Trefethen, employed by the Wildlife Management Institute, an organization funded by sporting-arms manufacturers. Even now Trefethen's book is the most comprehensive study of its subject, though important works by Thomas Dunlap and Lisa Mighetto have brought to light the efforts of biologists and humanitarians on behalf of wildlife. The most emphatic case for the hunters, however, came from John Reiger, who went so far as to maintain that conservation was *invented* by sportsmen, not biologists, not foresters, not impractical Romantics. Sportsmen provided the critical support for setting aside and protecting national parks and national forests, he claimed, and they were the first to promote the awareness of resource exhaustibility and the ideal of a more sustainable society for America.[24]

Reiger's main purpose, however, was to defend sport hunting as an ethical activity. To do that he tried to show that conservation as a reform movement emerged out of the sport hunter's "code," derived from English landed gentry. The code taught that there were fair and foul means of taking an animal's life—that there were ethical norms in hunting. More importantly for conservation, the sportsman's code suggested that all commercial hunting should be forbidden. Since most of the wildlife slaughter had been done by commercial hunters in order to sell vast quantities of meat, hides, furs, and feathers in the market, they were the ones to be stopped; it was they, not the sportsmen, who were threatening species with extinction. Denying the legitimacy of market hunting was the first step toward saving wildlife, but it led on to deeper doubts about fundamental American economic ideas and institutions. To criticize market hunting was to criticize what Reiger calls "capitalist democracy," the notion that the free, egalitarian, and unregulated pursuit of wealth must lead to the welfare of all. A world devoid of wildlife, however, was what capitalism really produced. Capitalist democracy was biocidal. Therefore it must be checked by laws, rules, and ethics, while that particularly malevolent manifestation of capitalism called the market hunter simply must go. The sportsman's code did not necessarily require the elimination of all forms of capitalism, admits Reiger, but it did work against its extension to wildlife, and it did lead many Americans to question, in fairly broad terms, the policy of laissez-faire and self-interest as the basis for humankind's relations with nature.

The leading figure in nineteenth-century wildlife conservation, and the most influential advocate of the sportsman's code, was George Bird Grinnell, a patrician New Yorker and a frequent visitor to, and for a while a rancher in, the American West. In 1880 Grinnell became the editor of the magazine *Forest and Stream*, in whose pages he began to inveigh against the "corruption of sport" and the subversion of all value by "the mighty dollar," a dollar that had become "the controlling agency in every branch of social and public life." Oddly enough Grinnell shared much of that dollar mentality of the business world, its rational accounting of profit and loss, its faith in the management of resources for greater production; but all the same, he resented the commercialism and Philistinism that was creeping across the nation and despoiling the environment and outdoor life. Like many patricians of his day, he was caught between allegiance to his social class and nostalgia for a premodern frontier life, when the Plains had been filled with Indians and buffalo. His way of resolving the conflict was to campaign pointedly against commercial hunting as an immoral enterprise. It was also unnecessary, he believed, in the modern age.

> The day of wild game as an economic factor in the food supply of the country has gone by. In these four hundred years we have so reduced the game and so improved and developed the other resources of the country that we can now supply food with the plow and reaper and the cattle ranges cheaper than it can be furnished with the rifle and the shotgun. In short, as a civilized people we are no longer in any degree dependent for our sustenance upon the resources and the methods of primitive man. No plea of necessity, of economy, of value as food, demands the marketing of game. If every market stall were to be swept of its game to-day, there would be no appreciable effect upon the food supply of the country.

Grinnell was making a complicated argument, perhaps too complicated for purely logical analysis or full understanding. He supported the clearing of the country for commercial agriculture (wiping out a great deal of animal habitat in the process) and even welcomed that agricultural progress, because it allowed America to abolish market hunting. He advocated sport hunting on whatever land was left, because it would at once allow a more primitive, preagricultural experience for sportsmen, while at the same time instilling a new, advanced ethic among them, an ethic of self-restraint in the use of nature (backed up, to be sure, by plenty of game laws and the power of the state). Whether it all made sense or not, such essentially was the reasoning the nation, as well as Grinnell, began to follow in the next phase of its wildlife policies.[25]

In 1900 the Lacey Act brought the federal government into wildlife conservation for the first time, by forbidding the interstate shipment of wild birds and mammals and their products taken in violation of state hunting laws. All western states and territories had by that date passed some laws. They had established fish and game commissions or hired wardens, though some like Kansas had not yet defined any hunting seasons even for deer or ducks, while many did not yet require any hunting licenses, and a few (Kansas, Oklahoma, Texas, New Mexico, and Nevada) had not begun to impose bag limits for any species. A treaty between the United States and Canada to protect migratory birds became the law of the land in 1918. By that point there was also a federal Bureau of Biological Survey, forerunner of the modern Fish and Wildlife Service, with a staff of scientists busy studying animal populations and identifying which ones needed conserving and which did not. From these and other developments, it was clear that commercial hunting was indeed on its way out, leaving the wildlife to sport hunters, just as Grinnell wanted.[26]

Whether, however, the triumphant sportsmen would practice moral restraint remained to be seen. Most hunters did not come from patrician circles and seemed to require extensive tutoring in the sportsman's code. Could a democratic society, which gave every sportsman an equal right to kill to the limits of the law and sent millions into the field with guns, contrary to more exclusive Old World hunting patterns, rely on the diffusion of hunting codes and ethics to the masses? Would noncommercial hunters accept restrictions on their recreation to preserve the game? Above all was there enough game left on which to practice a sportsmen's code? Grinnell and his associates were prescient enough to realize that outlawing the market hunter or passing treaties and laws to restrain the sportsman was not enough; there were too many who sought the pleasures of the chase and too few animals left to satisfy them. Somehow the animals had to recover their stocks and be sufficiently abundant to meet the hunting demands of the nation, and that required attention to the possibilities of wildlife propagation.

By the twenties and thirties, the idea was emerging that Americans could learn how to propagate wild-animal populations in sufficient supply to meet the country's growing need for outdoor recreation. If the land could produce a cornucopia of food crops, it could also produce a plenitude of wild animals, and by some of the same methods of intelligent agronomy. That idea began to emerge as a moral imperative, a social ethic of producing wildlife to the highest practical level. Models for the ethic were the European nations that had long ago established "game administrations" to protect their own dwindling resources. As the executive committee of the Boone and Crockett Club explained in 1925, "the administration of game is nothing more than the plain common sense management of it so as to ensure a permanent breeding stock which will perpetually produce a given surplus." They went on to suggest that such management, "although vastly more complex and difficult," is similar to "the simpler one of the management of cattle or chicken ranches." The goal ought not to be the preservation of animals out of some theory that they had an inherent right to exist, but rather because human beings wanted them around. Two of the club's oldest leaders, George Grinnell and Charles Sheldon, argued that "animals are for man's use, and one of these uses is recreation, of which hunting is a wholesome form."[27]

The advocates of this wildlife-production ethic were self-proclaimed utilitarians (though not Benthamite utilitarians, for they disagreed with Bentham that it was a moral necessity to try to prevent any animal's suffering). They advocated intensified production in both agriculture and wildlife management and sought to reconcile those goals. Where they had once deemed the slaughter of the bison as "a mercenary and wanton butchery," they now saw that "the extermination was a necessary part of the development of the country." It served the production ethic by making the West available for raising crops that helped to feed a hungry world. Utilitarianism in wildlife policy, therefore, meant seeking not the return of bison or elk or waterfowl to all or even most of their former range, but rather the production of new stocks in strictly limited areas to serve human wants—wants that might complement rather than compete with the production of food. To that end the club urged the nation to acquire, reserve, and restore habitat where it could and propagate on them the most desirable animals. That habitat might be on public or on private land, though mainly it should be the government's responsibility to lead the way.

So a nationwide wildlife-refuge system came into being, though "refuge" never quite expressed the real, controlling purpose or ethic. Refuge suggested a place of protection from human demands, a place where animals could go to save their lives, where they would not be shot—whereas in fact the refuges became places where animals could get "administered" and even "harvested." Refuge managers built dams and dikes to impound water artificially, they sowed and reaped crops with standard farm machinery to attract wildlife, they allowed cattle to graze, and they invited in sportsmen. Antihunting critics like William Hornaday called the refuges "slaughter pens," for they had the effect of collecting wild animals in them for hunters to shoot; nonetheless, the time had come for refuges. Tiny Pelican Island off the coast of Florida, set aside by President Theodore Roosevelt in 1903, was the first officially designated refuge. The first created specifically for big-game animals was the National Bison Range, an area of 12,800 acres carved out of the Flathead Indian Reservation in Montana in 1909. A far more important date, however, was 1929, when the Migratory Bird Conservation Act authorized the government to buy habitat for wildlife conservation purposes, not merely reserve it out of the existing federal domain. With that act an organized system of refuges arrived and began to grow at a rapid rate. Already the federal government had designated 4.8 million acres as refuges (4.1 million of them in Alaska), including the elk range of Jackson Hole, Wyoming, and the antelope range of northern Nevada. In the ensuing decade of the 1930s, it would add 8.7 million more acres within the continental United States, most of that acreage lying in the Mississippi River valley, a critical flyway for migrating ducks and geese. By the thirties American farmers, long urged to produce to the maximum, were producing far more commodities than they could sell; therefore, farm production must be rolled back. That was good news for many vulnerable species, for land taken out of production could be turned into refuges. Critics again complained, this time that the standard method of purchasing such lands was through selling duck stamps (a kind of hunting permit) to hunters and taxing ammunition, which necessarily meant that those who controlled the refuges were those who paid the acquisition and administrative costs, that is, sportsmen. Nonetheless the refuges served well their purpose of propagating many forms of wildlife, and depleted populations began to rebound somewhat from their low estate.[28]

The presidential administration of Franklin Delano Roosevelt rightly gets credit for saving the unemployed, the aged, the banks and businesses from the Great Depression, for saving Indians from a cultural twilight through tribal revitalization, and for creating a permanent safety net for agriculture. Much less noticed has been its saving of the fauna of the American West and other regions. No other decade or administration did so much to save wildlife. By and large, however, the decade of the thirties did not see any official redefinition of the purpose underlying faunal conservation. The justification for saving animals continued to be based, as it was in the earlier part of the century, on the extent of their contribution to human welfare; and in determining that contribution, economic criteria continued to rank first, recreational criteria a growing second, and aesthetic or ethical criteria a distant last. Thus any animal that threatened any part of the embattled national or regional economy might still vanish.[29]

Unsurprisingly then, even with all the new wildlife conservation going on, some animals prospered, while others continued to die. Those that died, and died in great numbers through the 1920s and 1930s, were the predators of the West. They died because they did what was in their nature to do—eat other animals. Unfortunately for them, the animals they had left to eat were mainly the private property of ranchers: those "spotted buffalo," whose proper destiny was the butcher shop. For a half century, domesticated range animals had been expanding into the vacuum left by the great wildlife holocaust. Cattle occupied the ecological niches left empty by the bison; sheep moved into those once occupied by the pronghorn. By the final decade of the nineteenth century, sheep numbered 40 million in the West, while cattle peaked later, in the 1920s, at 15 million head. Most grazed the rangelands for some part of the year, even those that spent much of their time in feedlots or on small farm pastures. "Altogether, the number of domestic animals on the ranges between 1890 and 1940 may have approached twice the values for wild ungulates in presettlement times," writes Frederic Wagner, "while domestic grazing pressures may have been half again those of the wild animals." The range was unquestionably overstocked. Too many cattle and sheep meant a loss of habitat for birds, fish, and other species, plant and animal, as well as for the remnant wild herbivores, justifying John Muir's angry response that they were "flocks of hoofed locust, sweeping over the ground like a fire, and trampling down every rod that escapes the plow." To prevent the West from becoming an ecological wasteland, the livestock needed culling, and the predators that had so far escaped a bullet fell to the work with gusto.[30]

Naturally the owners of livestock did not see matters from the wolf's point of view, or for that matter from an ecologist's. Some of those owners sat on House and Senate agricultural committees, men like John Kendrick of Wyoming, a cattleman, and John Thomas of Idaho, a sheepman, and they were in a position to get government help in a war to exterminate all the predators, adding for good measure all the rodents that dug holes on the range that sheep might stumble into. In 1915 Congress ordered the Bureau of Biological Survey to undertake an extermination program, using guns, steel traps, and strychnine-laced carcasses to rid the range of all undesirable animals, especially the coyotes that preyed on sheep and lambs.

Wyoming furnishes a representative case of that program's effectiveness. A dozen hunters went out to "clean up" the offending species, as though they were dirt to be swept out the door. The hunters gave names to particular animals, suggesting their pariah status: Scar-Face, Five-Toes, Three-Toes, Two-Toes (apparently the traps were doing their work), Big-Foot, Red Flash, and most notorious of all, the Custer Wolf, "king of the outlaws," a cunning beast that ran with "a bodyguard of two coyotes" before taking a bullet in the head. In the years 1916–28, the federal hunters, aided by state government and local stockmen association employees, wiped out over 40,000 animals in Wyoming, along with an estimated 20,000 that were poisoned but never found. Over half of those killed were coyotes, but there were also 18 mountain lions, 706 wolves, 169 bears, 1,524 bobcats, and 31 lynxes. Putting poison baits out had the unfortunate side effect of killing other, nontarget animals, such as furbearers and ranch dogs. Poison was also used against prairie dogs, ground squirrels, pocket gophers, jack rabbits, and rats "infesting Wyoming in great numbers," eating up the native grasses and cultivated crops; the federal government distributed in those years 363 tons of poisoned bait to eliminate all those "vermin" once and for all. As the prairie dogs died, so also died species dependent on them, such as the black-footed ferret. Even the beautiful magpies had to be destroyed, for they attacked song and game birds that the ranchers liked. The BBS drilled holes in sticks, packed them with poisoned ground suet, and placed them high in the trees, where the magpies would find them. All this was done in the pursuit of "harmony" on the range. "Our modern civilization," wrote government officials, "requires that we harmonize as nearly as possible the lives of our wild native animals with our agricultural activities. This calls for the protection and preservation of elk, deer, antelope, moose, mountain sheep, and other valuable forms of wild life. To do this, we must eliminate certain predatory animals that prey upon those wild mammals that we consider beneficial, and on domestic stock. The control of rodents is necessary to produce forage and crops."[31]

Poisoning wildlife in the name of conservation may seem a strange idea to another generation—conservation as carnage, bringing the smell of decaying bodies everywhere—but it was perfectly comprehensible in terms of the ethic that had evolved out of George Bird Grinnell's sporting code. That ethic again was one of producing game for hunters, much as ranchers produced domestic livestock. On that theme of increased production of whatever was useful, both hunters and antihunters could agree completely, as they could on the necessity of removing all species that interfered with such production. William Hornaday, for example, though a radical wildlife preservationist, was as hostile toward predators as any deer hunter or sheepman; "the coyote," he wrote, "is an Ishmaelite ...and should be killed wherever found in a wild state." Even many birds, like the golden eagle and the peregrine falcon, were obstacles to harmony; so "wicked" and "totally depraved" were they that they deserved nothing less than the death sentence. Their crime was that they preyed on "innocent" creatures useful to society. The ethic of conservation, consequently, put them in the same category as the old "game hogs," the frontier riffraff, the debased humans who had once killed so indiscriminately, so selfishly. Conservation demanded a code of restraint against wanton human violence, but it also insisted that anyone or anything that reduced the productivity of the land be stopped dead in its tracks. In the name of this ethic, the government spent millions of dollars on "animal control"—and thereby left another layer of skulls and bones scattered across the western landscape.[32]

Typical of the game managers of the Grinnell school was Elliott Barker of New Mexico, who alternated between federal resource agencies and private ranching with ease. Employed by the U.S. Forest Service for a decade, he came to know well the Pecos headwaters area on the east side of the Sangre de Cristo mountain range, fabled for its lost gold mines and buried treasure (the area became part of the Santa Fe National Forest), and then the Carson National Forest, farther north in the state. When he left the service, he raised cattle for a time until forced out of business by the crash of 1929. After that he became a predatory- animal hunter and game manager on a private estate near the Colorado border. All along his principal ambition had been to rid the country of the last few mountain lions and grizzly bears, which were taking the deer, elk, and cattle that humans wanted. Barker, it must be said, felt little of the moral indignation against predators that men like Hornaday did; indeed, he was sentimentally attached to his victims, exterminating them with some reluctance. "One heaves a great sigh of regret that the noble grizzly is gone—I fear forever—because the country must be kept safe for livestock." The production of meat, however, was for him an overriding cause, and he made himself its skillful instrument. In 1931 Barker became New Mexico's chief game warden, a position that allowed him to push conservation-as-useful-production thinking far and wide across the state.[33]

For expert guidance on what a state warden must do, Barker would undoubtedly have turned to the man who, more than any other, invented the profession of wildlife or game management, Aldo Leopold, a district forest supervisor in New Mexico. Barker had served under Leopold in the Carson and had been his deputy in the New Mexico Game Protective Association. Early on he must have read Leopold's essay on "The Varmint Question," which called for an alliance of stockmen and game protectionists to eradicate predatory animals. They were eating "the cream off the stock grower's profits," Leopold wrote, "and it hardly needs to be argued that, with our game supply as low as it is, a reduction in the predatory animal population is bound to help the situation." Nearly two decades later, when Barker had become state warden and Leopold was sitting in an academic chair at the University of Wisconsin, the teacher explained once more what the production ethic meant. "Game management," wrote Leopold in the first sentence of a book with that title, "is the art of making land produce sustained annual crops of wild game for recreational use." Like the agricultural arts of farming, ranching, or forestry, game management "produces a crop by controlling the environmental factors which hold down the natural increase, or productivity, of the seed stock." Regarded in that light, there need be no fundamental conflict among the different kinds of land managers. They all could unite in a war against animals interfering with production—insects, predators, rodents—while making sure that the desirable ones increased.[34]

By the 1930s Leopold, Barker, and other wildlife enthusiasts could look back with satisfaction on a great deal of progress toward achieving that enhanced production goal. There were now plenty of laws restricting hunting, hefty federal appropriations for removing predators, a growing system of refuges and parks for propagating new stock, and the beginnings of cooperation between agriculture and wildlife interests on growing food and cover for threatened game. A 1938 census by the BBS showed nearly 6 million big-game animals dwelling in the country, most of them in the western states, except for the Virginia or white-tailed deer, the most numerous of all the hunted species and an animal particularly adapted to disturbed landscapes. The elk population had climbed to more than 200,000, the bighorn to nearly 20,000, the mule deer to 1.5 million, the peccary to 40,000, the bison to 4,500.[35] Though those figures looked small compared to the numbers of livestock that had shouldered in, and small compared to the wild numbers present in the days of Lewis and Clark, they were large enough to make extinction no longer imminent. Apparently a gigantic industrial nation could live compatibly with a remnant wild fauna, though not with bears, lions, or wolves. In the fall seasons, great V's of geese could go on flying south, and hunters could be assured of enough of them to fill the home larder. The West, poised on the edge of massive demographic change in its towns and cities, could now expect to see forever some of the same game species that Black Elk once knew. The price of that success, however, was that the animals must now lead extensively managed lives, carefully selected and propagated for the hunt, controlled over their whole territory and life cycle to varying degrees of precision, dependent on human demand for their very existence, kept in check by recreational hunters rather than by other species. What were such animals in truth? Were they now only a marginally wilder version of domesticated cattle? Were they like sheep led to the slaughter, chickens raised for every pot? What then was tame and what was wild? What was the end or purpose of this management, and was it morally defensible? Whose interests did it serve? Those were the kind of questions that leaders like Aldo Leopold pushed to the edges of their minds for a while to concentrate on the pressing work of restoration. The questions would come back, however, to perplex the West and its wildlife experts in the decades ahead.

In 1934, one year after publishing his landmark textbook on game management, Aldo Leopold admitted, "In the long run we shall learn that there is no such thing as forestry, no such thing as game management. The only reality is an intelligent respect for, and adjustment to, the inherent tendency of land to produce life."[36] That was a strange comment from a man who had just spent several decades in developing game management and had just written the great bible in the field, a man whom hundreds of young professionals had begun to call "father." It must have been a puzzling statement for many who had just begun to learn the ethic and techniques of producing a crop of deer. Now, Leopold was saying, they must understand that they could not really *produce* game. The problem was too complex. Wild animals are not a commodity resembling those a farmer produces as he clears, plants, and tills a field; they can only be the spontaneous product of the land, arising out of the self-regulating, self-renewing capacities of life itself, and that fact makes the game manager's role quite unlike a farmer's. If healthy, the land does not really need any managers to carry out its processes; it needs them only to prevent interference by other humans who would make the land unhealthy.

Leopold has been one of the two or three most important figures in twentieth-century American conservation thinking, and the shift that he was signaling here in his approach to wildlife would be the pivotal one for post-World War II conservation generally. It might be described as a shift away from an ethos focused on sustained production of resources, selected according to human demands, to one of respectful accommodation to the land as a collective, interdependent entity. Nature, he was now saying, forms a self-renewing whole that humans must appreciate and adjust to. The idea began to surface in Leopold's own mind in the mid-1930s, though it had been anticipated much earlier by figures like John Muir; then after the war it spread rapidly among many sectors of the public. Along with the realization that modern humans have a global impact on nature, this new ethos has become the dominant theme in advanced environmental thinking.

In a 1944 report that has only recently appeared in print, Leopold called for an entirely new "system of thought" based on what he called "the concept of land-as-a-whole." Instead of thinking about game or fish as separate commodities, as discrete populations in which humans had a material interest, conservationists needed to see the land as a single complex entity. "Conservation is usually thought of as dealing with the supply of resources," he wrote, and he might have been describing himself at an earlier point. "This 'famine concept' is inadequate, for a deficit in the supply of any given resource does not necessarily denote lack of health, while a failure of function always does, no matter how ample the supply." It was possible, he now realized, for game managers to produce an abundant supply of shootable wildlife on land that was sick. The land might be overflowing with deer, but all the other wildlife might be gone and the land declining or endangered by that very abundance; the vegetation might be overbrowsed, the soil might be eroding, the streams filled with silt. Perceiving that broader entity of the land and safeguarding its health should be the dominant purpose of conservation.

Most people, unfortunately, had never seen land in a state of health, for that condition disappeared with the coming of the whites and their agriculture; achieving a state of health, therefore, must first depend on imagining what had not existed for a long time. Leopold did not insist that land health be defined in terms of restoring the full original flora and fauna, a definition that would simply condemn all changes made by Americans to the continent and would make the ideal of health a hopeless goal; rather, he spoke of preserving "the capacity for self-renewal in the soils, waters, plants, and animals that collectively comprise the land." Of course the land had to be modified, but it should be modified "as gently and as little as possible." Lose the soil and you lose the capacity for life itself; lose the watershed, ditto. Lose the seed stock for all the plants and animals, and the land must wait a million years to evolve a new biota. This reconceptualization of conservation as working back toward a healthy land, a self-renewing land, and repairing any aggressive, violent change, had profound implications for the West, as it did for other regions. Leopold would have Americans understand and follow "the unity concept" in nature: that is, they should deal with nature as a whole rather than as parts. The hunter should not concentrate only on obtaining a supply of elk meat but understand that elk are the natural product of a mountain meadow in a state of health. The bird watcher should not work to save the whooping crane while ignoring the health of wetlands. The cattleman should see that he cannot for long raise livestock in a land that has been radically destabilized and depleted of its interrelated complexity of plant and animal life.[37]

Why Leopold suddenly began to think in those terms, or for that matter, why so many conservationists followed him, is an important question to answer, for it goes right to the heart of an important shift in American culture. One of the leading authorities on Leopold's life and thought, Susan Flader, has suggested three experiences that he went through in the critical year of 1935, eight years after he had left New Mexico for Madison, Wisconsin. In that year he helped found the Wilderness Society to protect relatively undisturbed natural areas he had helped identify in the national forests and other public lands of the West.[38] He also acquired an abandoned farm on the Wisconsin River and began trying to restore it to health. And in that same year he traveled to Germany to study forestry and wildlife-management methods, which so bothered him with their artificiality that he came home determined to promote a more natural kind of management here.[39]

Flader also mentions that it was in the mid-1930s that Leopold began to read widely in the emerging science of ecology, which raised his consciousness from the level of single, discrete game populations to the whole interrelated biota. Trained in forestry, self-tutored in game management, Leopold now became an applied ecologist, reading the leading theorists in the field and drawing from them radical new insights about managing forests and wildlife. The "unity concept" was itself informed by ecology. In another essay, "A Biotic View of the Land," published in 1939, he pointed out the unsettling implications in ecology for traditional wildlife managers:

> The emergence of ecology has placed the economic biologist in a
> peculiar dilemma: with one hand he points out the accumulated
> findings of his search for utility, or lack of utility, in this or that species;

with the other he lifts the veil from a biota so complex, so conditioned by interwoven cooperations and competitions, that no man can say where utility begins and ends. No species can be "rated" without the tongue in the cheek; the old categories of "useful" and "harmful" have validity only as conditioned by time, place, and circumstance. The only sure conclusion is that the biota as a whole is useful, and biota includes not only plants and animals, but soils and waters as well.[40]

One startling implication in the new science was that all those predators ("varmints") that Leopold had once sought to kill must now be seen as integral parts of the biota, as useful to the whole as the animals they preyed on; in fact, from the point of view of the land as a whole, having plenty of predators meant enjoying a state of supreme health. To rid the Southwest of grizzlies and mountain lions, as Elliott Barker was still trying to do, was to kill the patient. Not all westerners agreed with that conclusion, of course, but those who did agree had gone through a similar shift in thinking about wild animals and were talking in ways that almost no one had done since white explorers had first come into the country.

I agree with Flader that those experiences of 1935, and that encounter with the new science of ecology, were decisive for Leopold, but they do not account completely for the change going on in his thinking. Another large reason had to do with the man's social imagination. He had become increasingly a critic of American individualism, particularly economic individualism, with its glorification of the pursuit of self-interest, of the profit motive, of private welfare at the expense of the community, and increasingly he sensed that conventional conservation thinking was still tainted by that outlook, particularly in its categorization of nature as either useful commodities or useless encumbrances. Wildlife policy may have come a long way since the days of unrestricted market hunting, but it was still based on satisfying consumer demand and human interest. The traditional policy lacked a holistic perspective toward nature because it lacked a holistic perspective on society. Seeing the whole, the land as a unity, depended on seeing the whole human community and being concerned about it.

That sense of connection between society and nature runs all through Leopold's writings in his years of profound reappraisal. Conservationists, he wrote in 1934, "are just beginning to realize that their task involves the reorganization of society, rather than the passage of some fish and game laws." What he had in mind was nothing less than replacing the old "rugged individualism" with a new social ethic, a communitarianism that placed the welfare of the human group above that of the individual. Ten years later he was sounding the same theme: "Unified conservation must ... be activated primarily as an obligation to the community, rather than as an opportunity for profit." "If conservation on private lands is to be motivated solely by profit, no unified conservation is even remotely possible." "In addition to being a conscious citizen of his political, social, and economic community," the landowner "should be a conscious citizen of his watershed, his migratory bird flyway, his biotic zone." The outcome of such reasoning was what Leopold called the "land ethic," first introduced in 1935 but given its fullest statement in the essay by that title he composed in 1947, just a few months before he died. A land ethic is essentially a moral obligation people have to maintain the whole of nature, and it requires a voluntary limitation on personal freedom and a transcendence of self-interest. As Leopold explained, it changes "the role of *Homo sapiens* from conqueror of the land-community to plain member and citizen of it. It implies respect for his fellow-members, and also respect for the community as such." An ethical relation to the land, Leopold had come to believe, cannot appear in a society that has no sense of mutual obligation or citizenship; our relations with nature are an extension of our relations with our fellow humans.[41]

Why did Leopold come to think this way? Apparently he had been so inclined for a long time, probably since his youth and certainly since the twenties, when again and again, even while serving as secretary of the Albuquerque Chamber of Commerce, he had expressed contempt for the culture of "boosterism," materialism, and "Babbittry" (a reference to Sinclair Lewis's satirical portrait of a businessman in *Babbitt*, 1922). I suspect that the Great Depression turned that inclination into a greater understanding of the need for communitarian values both in his political and conservation thinking. The thirties was a decade when many Americans repudiated economic individualism and turned toward more inclusive, collective attitudes, in some cases demanding that the government take on a larger role in helping the disadvantaged, in others taking on more responsibility themselves for the common welfare. Leopold was never very open about his politics, nor did he make many direct comments on the economic and political conditions of the times. His son Luna recalled that he was not impressed by either of the major parties in the 1930s and 1940s and voted for Norman Thomas, the socialist presidential candidate. But if that was how he voted, it did not get mentioned in his writings. Politics, socialist or otherwise, did not occupy much of his attention. He tended to the view that it was the individual's

responsibility, not the government's, to achieve "unified conservation"—though his emphasis was decidedly on the individual's "responsibility," not on the individual's rights. Still the land ethic had a clear
political dimension, resting as it did on a repudiation of the core ethos of
capitalistic economics and politics and requiring, as Leopold put it, "a
limitation on freedom of action in the struggle for existence" and an
extension of cooperation to all forms of life.[42]

Since his death in 1947, Leopold's vision of a wildlife policy grounded
in a more holistic understanding of the land has probably had more effect
on the public than on professionals, and more on nonlandowners than
landowners. Leopold's last book, *A Sand County Almanac*, has sold more
than a million copies, and his idea of a "land ethic" has spread widely in
popular thinking, suggesting that a majority of those who pay serious
attention to environmental issues today are Leopoldian, supporting not
only his tolerant, inclusive attitude toward all wild animals, game or not,
but also his vision of citizenship in both a social and ecological sense. On
the other hand, a substantial percentage of wildlife professionals continue to follow the early instead of the late Leopold. State wildlife
budgets still devote only a tiny fraction of their funds to nongame species.
Management of wild populations often follows aggressive, manipulative,
and interfering methods rather than a "let nature take its course"
philosophy. Many wildlife experts have come to believe, naturally
enough, that nature *needs* them and their expertise; it is they who keep
the place "healthy," "rational," "balanced," and "productive," all qualities that nature alone cannot achieve. Professionals may talk a lot about
ecology, but their ecological science often has little relation to Leopold's
understanding of the need to restore complex unity to the landscape. As
for private landowners, the evidence seems clear that most are far from
adopting a genuine land ethic. Farmers in particular are working their
acres more intensively than ever, still eliminating wildlife habitat
(prairie potholes, for example, vital to waterfowl), letting soils erode,
drastically rearranging waterways, trusting in technology more than in
nature. Taken together, the professionals and the private landowners are
a tiny part of the American public, but it is a part with enormous power.
Offsetting them is the much larger group who influence national environmental legislation, and it is at that level that one finds a perceptible
shift toward Leopold's point of view.[43]

That shift is most obvious on the public lands where private landowner
rights do not interfere. On wildlife refuges, in the national parks and
forests, and to a much lesser extent across the entire public domain,

officials have moved—slowly, sometimes resistingly—toward a philosophy of preserving ecosystems, including the whole biota, rather than
individual, favored species. No one played a more important role in that
development than Leopold's eldest son, Starker, a distinguished wildlife
biologist at the University of California at Berkeley. In a time of
fundamental reevaluation of policy, Secretary of the Interior Stewart
Udall named Starker the chairman of an Advisory Committee on
Wildlife Management, and it produced three separate, influential reports: one on the national parks (1963), one on predator and rodent
control (1964), and one on the national refuge system (1968). All of
them promoted the ideal of "natural ecosystem management," which
meant that the managers should stop manipulating the biota to favor the
most appealing and charismatic fauna, or the most useful, or the most
demanded by hunters, or the least threatening to stock growers. To the
greatest extent practical, they should preserve all native species in at
least minimal numbers. The coyote deserved a place in the landscape, as
did all the predators, even if sheep had to be protected from their
depredations. Within the parks the native biotic associations—not
merely discrete species, but their associations—"should be maintained,
or where necessary re-created, as nearly as possible in the conditions that
prevailed when the area was first visited by the white man." Accommo-
dating tourists in the parks should become less important than maintaining the original biota. Similarly the refuges should be vignettes of a lost,
wild America: "We view each National Wildlife Refuge in the old-
fashioned sense of a bit of natural landscape where the full spectrum of
native wildlife may find food, shelter, protection and a home. It should
be a place where the outdoor public can come to see wild birds and
mammals in variety and abundance compatible with the refuge environment. It should be a 'wildlife display' in the most comprehensive sense."
These words appealed to the public as well as the Interior Department,
and under their influence public-land management began to seek a new
course, even on lands long devoted to producing profitable commodities,
such as minerals, meat, and lumber.[44]

Still another manifestation of the Leopold legacy was the passage in
1973 of the Endangered Species Act, the most radical piece of environmental legislation ever passed in the United States. Basically the act said
that no species should be allowed to go extinct by human hands.
Suddenly hundreds of species, ranging in the western states from gray
wolves to desert tortoises, Chinook salmon, whooping cranes, silverspot
butterflies, California condors, and northern spotted owls, became

morally as well as scientifically significant. Although the legislation suggested that each of these species had an incalculable value, and saving them was not to be reduced to a matter of cost-benefit analysis, in actuality congressional appropriations to implement the act did provide an economic index to public commitment. By 1990 the government was spending $102 million a year on endangered and threatened species, half of that amount going to twelve species identified as especially "significant." Never mind for the moment how that significance got decided. Never mind how well the act was administered by an Interior Department that, between 1981 and 1992, was distinctly hostile to noneconomic values. Never mind that a hundred million dollars was less than a single block-buster movie took in at the box office. Never mind that Leopold would undoubtedly have wanted to devote that money to saving whole ecosystems rather than particular endangered species, even if it meant invading private-property rights. Grant only that the passage of the act represented a dramatic turnaround in wildlife policy, away from the production ethic that preoccupied the public for a long while and still survives tenaciously today in many groups, and toward the broader goals, the ethical principles, that Leopold came to hold. To paraphrase him, we have at least drawn nearer the point of admitting that all species should continue as a matter of biotic right, regardless of what they offer us in the way of economic advantage.[45]

This is not the place to survey the entire postwar environmental movement, or all the contemporary controversies over wildlife and ecology, or even the battles currently going on in the American West between preservationists and developers, free-market proponents who would privatize all wildlife and "deep ecologists" who would give equal rights to all species, from bacteria to humans. I will only note the increasing role of women in this debate over wild things, a role that may alter significantly the issues and the manner of their discussion. With few ties to the hunting tradition or sportsman's code, and with shrinking ones to farming or other extractive industries, modern women may represent a fresh perspective on the human-animal relation. Rachel Carson, for example, who stands with Leopold as the other great formative influence on environmentalism, went beyond him in expressing a reverence for life. The two would surely have agreed on the danger posed by pesticides to the land and on the need for a unified ecological approach to preserve a healthy earth, yet Carson was more ready to see suffering—to feel deep within her the pain of an animal, to feel it as her own pain. Other women have tended to follow her example and have become not only activists in environmental causes, fighting against toxic threats to health, for instance, but also activists in the animal-rights movement, which in recent years has sprung back to life and is now beginning to challenge many wildlife policies.[46] The ideas behind the movement are old, going back to Jeremy Bentham and Henry Bergh, but recently it has been women who have been especially active in reviving and extending those ideas from the protection of domesticated stock and laboratory-research victims to wilderness creatures, often insisting that all uses of all animals are wrong. The final outcome of this movement, the impact it will have on hunting, trapping, ranching, and even real-estate development, cannot be predicted. What can be said is that women, especially well-educated urban women, have now found a powerful voice, and it is speaking with new vigor about the obligations and courtesies we owe the animals, the other people in our lives.[47]

Since Lewis and Clark shot their first grizzly in 1804, the West has been a place where Americans have come to kill animals as well as raise and preserve them. Today most of the national debates over wildlife policy—regarding predators, refuges, parks, and endangered species—are also about specific places in the West and about who has a right to live there. The region stands at the center of a national, and an international, dialogue over the fate of those other beings, those other people and nations, so like us humans, so fatally different. The animals, of course, do not enter into that dialogue, or if they speak, we cannot hear them. Those who do the talking are all human beings, discussing with one another what to do with and for thousands (and globally millions) of species. So far the dialogue has been bitterly divided. If we have trouble agreeing on what human languages, values, and ethnicities "belong" in the West, we have even more difficulty agreeing on the desirability of those other people. They seem so alien, so destructive at times, so out of place in some of our visions, that some of us still wish them dead. Others insist that the West can, and indeed must, include in its sense of community the likes of spotted owls and howling wolves, all the flying people, the swimming people, the crawling people, the walking people once accepted and respected by the two-leggeds who possessed the land. What is at stake is nothing less than the notion of community that we want to nurture henceforth in the West.

4

------◆------

The Warming of the West

The Great Plains may look like a simple problem, but they are not. Despite their seeming monotony of flat immutable land meeting big unchanging sky, they are in fact the most volatile place on the North American continent. Their complexity lies not in landforms, which offer so little visual variety, but in climate. Nowhere else do Americans confront such extremes of cold and hot, or such rapid oscillations around the crucial point that divides wet from dry.

The old pioneer song brags about how steady and cheerful is our home on the range, "where the skies are not cloudy all day," "where seldom is heard a discouraging word," "where the deer and the antelope play." But we know that the man who wrote that song must have been heavily editing his data. Deer and antelope *at play* in the fields of eastern Colorado, on a gentle *frolic* across the Staked Plains of Texas? The song leaves out the flies and scummy waterholes, the hard winters the animals regularly endured. Today the deer that have survived the trauma of invading white civilization are probably choking on tractor dust or getting drenched by center-pivot irrigation systems. We have to admit too that dark clouds hang over the Plains from time to time, and now and then they carry no water at all; they are full of dust. And as for no discouraging words, in fact the Plains have heard many such words over the past century: words full of human grief, words expressing anger, surprise, disillusionment, words profane and obscene.

The stark truth is that the Plains have been an endless puzzle and a considerable disappointment to those who have tried to tame them. We have never really understood them well, and we have seldom been realistic about their possibilities.

Over the next hundred years, the words may get more discouraging than ever, if climatologists are right. Planet Earth is beginning to warm up, and the Plains are going to get more than their share of the warmth. The Intergovernmental Panel on Climate Change, a large, distinguished group of scientists assembled by the World Meteorological Organization and the United Nations Environment Programme, has calculated that the global mean temperature will rise 3 degrees Centigrade before the end of the twenty-first century, if no radical changes occur in technology and human behavior, and if we continue on our present course of polluting the atmosphere freely with carbon. Those three little degrees would constitute a greater atmospheric change than we have seen over the past ten thousand years, and it would come far more rapidly than any remotely comparable change in the history of civilization.[1]

The panel goes on to predict that "temperature increases in . . . central North America" will be "higher than the global mean, accompanied on average by reduced summer precipitation and soil moisture."[2] Now they are referring directly to the Great Plains, along with the upper Mississippi River valley—essentially all the states from Indiana west to Colorado. Though no one can be quite sure what the specific regional effects of global warming will be, most qualified observers agree with that prediction. In effect the area will be returning to and exceeding the conditions existing during the mid-Holocene Altithermal (or Hypsithermal) Period of some five to eight thousand years ago, when mean temperatures in the middle latitudes were 1.5 to 2.5 degrees Centigrade higher than today, when the present U.S. corn belt was a dry prairie and the western wheat belt was a near desert.[3] Other scientists expect to see a similar trend toward increasing aridity showing up across the already arid Southwest and into California. Across much of the future American West, beginning about the years 2005 to 2020, we may expect a warmer climate than we are used to, and, beginning about the year 2030, less rainfall during the growing season and less soil moisture for raising our crops.[4]

How little do we understand the complicated forces, natural and now human induced, roiling the sky overhead. Who would have thought in the days of the sodbuster fighting off grasshoppers or of the cavalryman dodging Indian arrows that *carbon* would one day be the greatest threat to rural security? But then the sodbuster did not imagine that his or her descendants and fellow countrymen would one day burn natural gas, coal, and oil, some of it derived from underfoot on the Plains, or that automobiles, tractors, combines, and irrigation pumps would one day be in widespread use, requiring those fuels in massive amounts.

The warming trend predicted by the scientists is the result mainly of extracting carbon buried deeply in the ground and putting it up into the air in the form of carbon dioxide. The nation's economy does that all the time; it could not do otherwise and survive. As part of that economy, the rural Plains economy burns fossil fuels at a ferocious rate. A typical Plains farmer consumes, directly and indirectly, thousands of gallons of gasoline a year. Winter wheat production, for example, requires the energy equivalent of about 0.6 barrel per acre (or 1.5 barrels per hectare), as do sorghum and soybean production. Irrigated sorghum requires 4.0 barrels per acre, irrigated corn 5.7 per acre. Each of those barrels has the energy equivalence of over 47 gallons of gasoline. Thus on a one-thousand-acre dryland wheat farm, the farmer may be burning 28,200 gallons of gasoline to produce a single annual crop, not to mention the energy needed to ship that wheat to a grain elevator, a flour mill, a bakery, a supermarket, a restaurant or kitchen. The farmer's ancestors did not foresee such an energy-intensive way of life, but he finds it completely natural and is loathe to give it up. In practicing that modern agriculture, however, he is unwittingly helping to create a desert in his grandchildren's future.[5]

So the words frequently heard around tomorrow's home on the range will be: Hotter and drier. No rain in sight. Not much rain last year either, or the year before. The ground has no plant cover, the wheat has not taken root, the wind is starting to blow the topsoil away.

Those were the same conditions prevailing in the infamous Dust Bowl years of the 1930s, when 100 million acres suffered from serious wind erosion, when nearly a billion tons of dirt blew in some years from farm to farm, even blew east toward New York and the Atlantic Ocean. "The prairie," observed a reader of the *Dallas Farm News* in 1939, "once the home of the deer, buffalo and antelope, is now the home of the Dust Bowl and the WPA." In some counties one in every three farmers drew a relief check from the WPA (the Works Progress Administration) or other federal agencies.[6] Drought produced crop failure, crop failure produced erosion, erosion produced poverty. What the scientists are now predicting is nothing less than the return of some of those Dust Bowl conditions, though on a more permanent basis.[7]

The future may see an inexorable desiccation, not a temporary drought of two or eight or even twenty years. The winter wheat belt, now located in the central and southern Plains, may gradually shift northeastward into Iowa, Minnesota, and Canada. That may seem like good news if you own land or a grain elevator there, but wheat is a less profitable crop per acre than corn, and the shifting of the wheat belt would mean the displacement of the corn belt and an overall decline in prosperity. Nor would it be good news for most plains farmers to watch the Chihuahan desert creep toward them, nor for the whole country or anybody overseas who depends on us for food.

The shift of the breadbasket northward will mean lower overall production of wheat in the United States. Americans will likely still have enough to eat, but we will have less and less to export to our major markets abroad, including the countries of the former Soviet Union and Japan. In 1990–91 we shipped 1.1 billion bushels of wheat overseas, or about half the total harvest. That level will probably not be maintained. As Karl Butzer writes, "the United States, now the world's major food exporter, will barely remain self-sufficient, while the Soviet Union will be heavily dependent upon food imports."[8] And as the central and southern grain areas succumb to permanent desiccation, then the total income from plains agriculture will decline, as will the ability of Americans to buy foreign-made goods and to pay for them with the products of our land. Other countries, such as Canada, may gain a comparative advantage over U.S. producers and shippers in the international grain trade. The people who once looked to us for a reliable source of nutrition may have to tighten their belts or seek other suppliers.[9]

Many plains residents will respond to these predictions with skepticism bordering on disdain. The scientists, they will argue, do not know enough to be sure—and of course they are right; scientists are extrapolating from incomplete data and calling for prudent measures in the face of vast uncertainties. Residents of the Plains will also insist that they can handle anything. Even if these predictions come true, they can adapt their crops and tools, and can survive whatever comes their way, as they have always done, as their ancestors did before them.

Such confidence has support from a few other scientific experts, including a panel appointed by the National Academy of Sciences, which recently has declared that, as the world gets warmer, Americans should be able to adjust their lives and agricultural production at reasonable cost. Although there was sharp dissent from that conclusion, the majority of the panelists were optimistic about the future survivability of agriculture and industry. They pointed out that humans have long managed to live both in polar and tropical climates, proving that we are an adaptable species. Farmers will adapt by diversifying their crops, finding new water supplies for them, and air-conditioning their houses.

"The capacity of humans to adapt," said the panel's chairman, Paul Waggoner of the Connecticut Agricultural Experiment Station, "is evident in the rapid technological, economic and political changes of the past 90 years." He recommends that people get ready to move from one region to another, taking their farm machinery with them, and that the government be prepared to give disaster aid to those most affected by the desiccation, while allowing the marketplace to enforce adaptation. Take all those precautionary measures, he maintains, and we should weather the future nicely.[10]

Those are precisely the kind of encouraging words people want to hear, and if they also encourage Americans to cut down on fossil fuel consumption and invest in new crop research, they are sensible. But they are also naive in their assumptions about how easy it is to adapt culture and institutions to change and about how resourceful the human mind is. Will people dwelling in rural Colorado readily move to Canada? Will adequate disaster aid always come, and come promptly, from taxpayers elsewhere? Will more freedom in the market economy make plains farmers better off, or put them at a competitive disadvantage with respect to farmers in other regions—and out of business? Can we reliably expect plant breeders to discover a miracle wheat that can grow without rain? Will consumers learn to eat some bioengineered, high-protein syrup made from prickly pears in a lab? And what can we really learn from the example of Eskimos adapting to cold and snow about what we must do to adapt our farming to a desiccated West? They took thousands of years to learn how to live with their limited resources. We, on the other hand, have only a few decades to make our adjustments—to discover what kind of population density, standard of living, and agronomy the region can support. A lot has to be invented quickly. The model of the Eskimo is, therefore, more inspirational than practical. We will not need igloos in the days ahead.

Moreover the happy notion that the last ninety years of experience with rapid change proves that everything will turn out all right is wildly misinformed about that history. In the first place, those years have not been all that glorious or successful. They have witnessed the rise of the United States to global economic supremacy, but then came the loss of that leadership to the Japanese and Germans, and in recent decades has come a dispiriting decline in living standards for most Americans. During those tumultuous years, crime has gone up, drug use up, divorce up, military armaments up—all of which might be seen as manifestations of failure to cope with modern life. The technologies that have appeared so bewilderingly over that span of time may have been more or less absorbed into our lives, but at what cost to our psyches and to the natural environment? All along the way, the adaptations to change have been far more difficult than the panel remembers. And the evidence of abandoned farmhouses and dwindling small towns on the Plains or of growing slums and social decay in the cities suggest that many people have not been able to make those adaptations at all. The road from 1900 to the present has required massive demographic dislocations, brought great human and ecological costs, and produced a sharp-toothed anxiety gnawing at our national self-confidence. Panels looking toward the future of global warming ought to remember the full truth of what we have been through already.

Will the next ninety years present an easier transition than the last, or will they see even more dislocations, a more rapid downward spiral of bust and decline, and many more human failures? If some people will be winners in the global warming era, who will be the losers? The Plains and other parts of the West are our most likely candidates in the United States for being losers. To what extent can they survive the coming trends and endure as living space? The past gives no comforting answers to those questions.

As a historian I recommend that the Connecticut agronomist and his fellow scientists avoid making shallow analogies with other peoples and times and seek the aid of my profession to help understand the complex story of how well we have adapted to change in the past. They might, for example, read more of the history of the Great Plains and ask what lessons it holds for the future. To be sure a warming trend that exceeds anything over the past ten thousand years stands outside history as we have known it. Nonetheless we do have considerable experience with drought to draw on—in the 1890s, the 1930s, and so forth. We can learn from that history what people went through in such periods, what they learned or did not learn about nature, how well they adapted and where they failed, and we can draw from that experience some insights for the years ahead.

So what are some lessons from the history of human settlement in this western region of North America? What attitudes did the dominant group of the past century, the white settlers, bring to this place? How successful have they been in adapting their institutions, technology, and thinking to the not so simple Great Plains?

The first lesson we should draw from the region's history is that it is hard to adapt to a climate that you do not fully understand or do not fully want to accept. This is a lesson that applies to experts and common people alike. Both groups have a long record of talking about the plains climate with more confidence than is warranted. Indeed the history of climate thinking in the region ought to give even the global-greenhouse modelers a pause or two as they refine their predictions.

Throughout the nineteenth century, the dominant image of the Great Plains bounced between two oversimplified abstractions, each of them naive, rigid, and epic in its implications. The Plains are a "Desert," said some of the earliest white travelers into the region; not at all, insisted others, they are a "Garden," achieved or in the making. The geographer Martyn Bowden has argued that the first of those abstractions was one favored by eastern elite opinion, expressed in gazetteers and topographical reports, but that the westward-moving "folk" in all their practical wisdom ignored the implied warning in the desert notion, the pessimism about the land's potential, and came to settle the country anyway. The experts had wanted to counteract the anarchic, unsettling impulses of American society by inventing a formidable desert on the western frontier. Their negative images of the environment, which dominated national thinking until 1860, thus had an ideological content: they exaggerated the harsh natural conditions in order to serve a conservative social end of restraining geographical mobility.[11]

Undoubtedly Bowden is right about the elite's manipulation of data, but the common people were driven by ideology as much as were their councilors of restraint. What the people moving west in covered wagons wanted was a land of unlimited economic opportunity—an abundance of free soil ready for free labor by free hands. They needed to create a climate that would support that dream, and so they chose to talk about the Plains as the "garden of the West." If the land was not yet gardenlike, able to support all their traditional crops, they would make it so with their plows and enterprise. By plowing the land, many argued, they would alter the climate, increasing precipitation by some mysterious process of physics. Rain would follow the moldboard plow. As Wright Morris puts it, "God and man, working in close collaboration, first settled and then improved God's country."[12] From the time the first pioneers arrived on the Plains, through the late 1870s and 1880s, that folk ideology of environmental amelioration became the dominant one in public discourse. Though it came from deep impulses in the nation's popular culture, which rejected the idea of any natural limits on economic aspirations, it managed to find support from some experts. By the eighties, in fact, the experts were almost all converts to climate reformism. Hardly anyone dared to classify the region as a veritable desert anymore, when millions had come believing that, given enough faith and technology, it could become a garden producing an overflowing cornucopia of food and wealth.

As the dust began to blow in 1932, however, that victorious image of the Plains as a garden-in-the-making was profoundly shaken. Climate suddenly seemed to be more treacherous than many settlers had supposed. They felt betrayed by providence, by nature, by the government, by railroad companies, by agronomists, by anyone who had encouraged them in their efforts to make the Plains say wheat instead of buffalo grass. The rest of the nation shared their sense of disappointment and has never quite recovered from it. Henceforth the climate of the Plains would become symbolic of a fickle, dark, threatening, dangerous, and undependable nature. The old confidence that nature was reliably on the side of America, eager to help in its own subjection and improvement, disappeared.

Since the dirty thirties, we have talked about and studied the matter of climate endlessly, but we have not yet achieved much understanding of its complexity, despite spending millions of dollars on scientific research. An exact, reliable science of the region's weather patterns has not yet appeared. Climate, it has been said, is only average weather; but what is that average, we still want to know. And even if we could define an average, what could that tell us about the specific weather we can expect tomorrow?

Until very recently the science of plains climatology has confidently promised that it could discover what nineteenth-century gazetteers and homesteaders wished for: a predictability in the climate that could be neatly categorized, so that a stable civilization could built on it. Nature must have a clear steady pattern, it has been assumed, offering us a clear, single norm even if we want to change it. That expectation has its roots in ancient ideas, going back to the Greeks, of a designed universe, a world that is rational and orderly in terms we humans can understand. Scientist after scientist has hoped that, because the earth turns regularly on its axis, runs smoothly in its orbit, behaves itself circumspectly as all planetary bodies must, the earth's weather must also be a predictable phenomenon. If we could only gather enough facts, we could locate those regularities in the climate, just as Newton precisely described the motions of the heavens.

Even before the Dust Bowl years, a number of scientists had begun to investigate weather records of the Plains, sure that they could find the stable order lurking behind the shifting veil of change. That order was neither "desert" nor "garden," they concluded, but something in between: call it "subhumid" (John Wesley Powell's phrase) or "semiarid," or "marginal," all labels that tried to define the region in reference to climates lying east or west, which were taken to be the norms. Failing to agree on the labels, the scientists found it difficult to derive even a stable quantitative description of plains climate. In 1941 following the dust storms, C. Warren Thornthwaite wrote that the "rainfall is scanty, averaging less than 20 inches annually except in the warmer southern portion, and only slightly more than 10 inches in the north." But then he admitted that the variability of that rainfall is great: "Almost everywhere the driest year brings less than 10 inches and the rainiest more than three times that much." For Thornthwaite those statistics meant that "permanent agricultural settlement based on the production of grain for export is not possible" and the region must turn to cattle ranching for a permanent economic base, supplementing the natural pasturage with irrigated feed crops.[13]

Before the Dust Bowl, another climatologist for the U.S. Weather Bureau, Joseph B. Kincer, had called the region "semi-productive," though he was confident that it might "contribute, in some measure, to the nation's [food] supply" by using windmills to pump underground water to irrigate gardens and small truck plats.[14] As for drought patterns, Kincer admitted that there had been "a marked lack in uniformity in the recurrence of droughty years" since the late nineteenth century. The years 1894–95 had been very dry in the north but not in the south. Other dry periods included 1910–11, 1917–18, and 1925–26, but in none of those cases were all the plains states affected equally.[15] Science repeatedly had trouble pinning this region down to a simple order or single economic uses.

Among the scientists who studied plains climate assiduously was the Nebraska ecologist Frederick Clements, who invented the idea of a "climax" plant community to characterize the native vegetation before the white invasion. The climax was supposed to be the end point of plant succession, when, after the pioneering species had entered and broken ground, the plant community matured and settled down to an equilibrium condition. Unfortunately for the theory, the climax stage was determined by climate, and climate, Clements had to acknowledge, did not manifest any final equilibrium stage. Droughts came and droughts went. That condition of instability threatened the theory of a steady state of plant life and threw the Plains back into ceaseless turmoil. Was there any order to be found in those droughts, Clements wondered, an order that the plant community had evolved to handle? Was drought regular? If it was, then farmers might follow the model of the native plants and anticipate the coming of drought, adapting their behavior as the plants did.

Clements thought he had found that key to order in the cycles of sunspots, dark blotches on the surface of the sun that are associated with magnetic fields and intensified solar activity. Regularly every eleven years (scientists now calculate one sunspot cycle of 11 years and another of 22) the sun bursts out with spots. Gathering rainfall records from all over the West, Clements thought he saw in them a pattern of increased sunspot activity correlating with drought, and one of minimum sunspot activity correlating with increased rainfall. For the rest of his life, he continued to collect such data in the hope of predicting exactly the natural rhythms of drought. If he could make those predictions firm, then he could help farmers devise "a scientific system of expansion and contraction."[16]

The notion that sunspots determine droughts is an idea traceable to the beginnings of modern astronomy, when telescopes were first trained on the sun. At first scientists expected to find that whenever sunspots were at their maximum number, indicating that the sun is at its hottest temperature, the atmosphere on the earth would be warmer and droughts more common. Fewer spots and a cooler sun, on the other hand, would produce a cooling in the earth's atmosphere and more rainfall and snow. To their astonishment, scientists found that the exact opposite was true! More sunspots tended to be associated with lower temperatures and fewer spots with higher ones. Eventually this counter-intuitive outcome was explained by the homely example of a person sitting before a hot fireplace in a room and feeling cold drafts blowing against her neck. But the lesson in that surprise was that there is no easy connection between what goes on within the sun's dynamo and what happens within the atmosphere of the earth. Many simply became discouraged with making any connection at all and gave up the project.[17]

One man who persisted in trying to concoct a sunspot theory was Ellsworth Huntington, a geographer at Yale who is still known for his argument that all civilization depends on a temperate climate zone. In 1914 Huntington published *The Climatic Factor as Illustrated in Arid America*, which may have been the source of Frederic Clements's fascination with sunspots; both men were associated with the Carnegie

Institution of Washington, which for a while was the major sponsor of ecological and climatological research in the American West. In turn Huntington was much influenced by the work of Andrew E. Douglass, founder of the tree-ring research center in Arizona; Douglass was sure he had data from Germany and California showing that trees grow in cycles corresponding to the sunspots.[18]

Since Huntington and Clements, other scientists have spent a lot of time and money chasing the same will-of-the-wisp. The sunspots do not, as it turns out, correlate exactly with drought, nor does their absence with precipitation, when one looks at the full record of plains climate. The strongest evidence for a twenty-two-year periodicity in drought exists for the short period from the 1890s to the 1970s, but before that the evidence is weak or nonexistent. A severe drought occurred in the 1750s, another in the 1820s, and then another in the 1860s, all of them more severe than that of the Dust Bowl years; in fact the thirties do not rank in the top five droughts known to have occurred since the early eighteenth century. Douglass's recent successors at the Laboratory of Tree-Ring Research have concluded that "drought appears to recur at ill-defined intervals of from 15 to 25 years," and they add that "whatever effect solar variability may have on drought, it is overwhelmed by other factors at particular locations."[19] What those other factors are, they leave unexplained, but undoubtedly they are far more complex and numerous than scientists have been able to plot. We may now know more about the mechanics of drought than we did a few decades ago, but because of the complexity of factors involved, we can still predict almost nothing from week to week.

Climate, we are now beginning to acknowledge, is so complicated a series of events that we may never be able to make predictions that a farmer can rely on. The sky we live under is in perpetual, random motion—is non-Newtonian after all. In the phrase of some contemporary meteorologists, the climate is innately "chaotic," which is not to say that it has no structure or pattern, but that its patterns are nonlinear, stochastic, and dependent on too many variables to locate simple order in it—the simple order that the old science of meteorology expected.[20] So argues one of the most influential students of the subject, Edward Lorenz of the Massachusetts Institute of Technology. "There is little question but what the real atmosphere is an irregular system," he has pointed out, and "the most obvious influence of irregularity is its limitation on the extent to which the weather may be predicted."[21] Despite a considerable increase in climate- and weather-research funding from the 1960s to the present, science is still unable to claim solid forecasting beyond about a week into the future, let alone anticipate drought cycles over a period of decades or centuries.

Even the predictions of global warming I have mentioned, though worked out by Cray computers programmed by many brilliant minds, must be taken with a few grains of salt. Scientists can calculate how much carbon we are putting into the atmosphere and what its effects would be in a simplified computer model, but they cannot say where all the carbon really goes—how much of it gets absorbed by the oceans, for example, or how much gets taken up by plants, or how much stays in the atmosphere, creating a kind of greenhouse over our heads.[22]

The history of climate thinking on the Plains, therefore, leaves one with a humble sense of the mind's inadequacy before nature. We run into big difficulties whenever we try to transcend our mental limits and locate some lasting truths, some overall picture of order in nature. Our perception of climate has always been distorted by ideology, by a will-to-believe in popular thinking, even by the scientist's faith in a comprehensible, rational order in the universe. If a hundred years of settler experience and systematic scientific investigation have still not given us any sure ability to predict droughts, how can we expect to prepare readily for that long desiccation that may lie ahead? The answer is, we cannot. We may go on looking for smaller bits of order and pattern that we can hope to isolate and understand. We can try to develop at all levels of society a more adequate awareness of the complexity of the causes of drought, both natural and anthropogenic. Above all, we can try to respect what we do not fully understand, which is most of the world around us. But having done all that, we cannot expect to make a smooth, easy adaptation of settlement, agriculture, or economy to a climate that will always be a turbulent chaos of cloud, heat, and gas.

A second lesson derivable from the past is that trying to control nature through technology is not an adequate or long-term approach to adaptation. If we try to rely on our mechanical ingenuity to get us through drought or permanent desiccation, or to establish harmony with the natural world, the outcome may be even more catastrophic. Adaptation, if it means to last, must be cultural and social as well as technological.

One of the most important documents ever published about the region appeared in 1936, *The Future of the Great Plains*, written by a committee appointed by President Franklin Roosevelt and headed by Lewis C. Gray of the Bureau of Agricultural Economics. No other study collected as much social and economic information about rural communities or understood so clearly the root causes of the Dust Bowl disaster. The causes, according to the report, lay primarily in attitudes of mind brought by settlers to the region, and it argued that the Plains' biggest challenge was not simply to endure until better times arrived, but to change those attitudes, no matter how deep-seated they were. Number one on their list of attitudes needing reform was the notion that "man conquers Nature." "It is an inherent characteristic of pioneering settlement to assume that Nature is something of which to take advantage and to exploit; that Nature can be shaped at will to man's convenience." We now know, they concluded, that "it is our ways, not Nature's, which can be changed."[23]

Since the 1930s people on the Plains have pretty consistently ignored that admonition and instead looked for quicker, easier solutions—for a simple technological "fix" that would not require any searching self-examination or moral reassessment. So far no fundamental reform of attitudes has taken place. The conquest of nature through technology is still the dominant way of thinking, though regularly one hears a few local admonitions to the contrary. As global warming commences, that same old faith in technology's ability to manage nature completely may continue and may lead to foolish investments in one expensive, short-lived panacea after another, wasting time and capital in a vain effort to postpone the ultimate day of climate reckoning.

The list of technological fixes that have already been tried on the Plains can be found in any conservation district's annual report, usually followed by the lament that not enough farmers have put them into practice, but with the hope that more will become converts soon. They include using a chisel-plow to break up compacted soils (soils compacted by heavy machines rolling over them, ruining their permeability); leaving crop residues on the ground to slow the wind's velocity; practicing no-tillage cropping, which does not stir up the soil; applying herbicides to keep weeds down on those no-tillage fields; adopting drought- tolerant crop varieties developed by university and corporate plant breeders; and building bench terraces to slow water runoff. All those techniques are ingenious ways of making the available precipitation go as far as possible; considered as expressions of thrift they are unexceptionable, like insulating the walls of one's house to keep the heat in and the cold out. But they have limits and drawbacks. They are not cheap to adopt, and the rate of adoption goes up or down depending on changing rural income. Most of them require burning more fossil fuel, not less—farmers must burn gasoline to conserve rainfall—and therefore they have a limited future as energy supplies decline. And like all technological fixes, they feed the dangerous illusion that nature has "been shaped at will to man's convenience."

The most important technology adopted since the 1930s has undoubtedly been deep-well irrigation. More than any other innovation, it has allowed the Plains to overcome the threat of severe drought and encouraged the confidence that water not only can be conserved but also can be "invented." If there is no water in sight, it can be found somewhere else and delivered. That notion was, of course, implicit in the old slogan "rain follows the plow," but by the thirties people were beginning to lose faith in the plow as a water maker and were looking for better mechanical saviors, for example, a steel pipe to bring water from a distant river or a reservoir. The Great Plains Committee warned that "the current popular emphasis on new supplies of water . . . by which irrigation farming may widely replace dry farming, rests on hopes inevitably doomed to disappointment. . . . Sound water- mindedness will recognize the basic facts of nature which man is powerless to alter."[24] The committee knew the checkered history of surface irrigation on the Plains, illustrated, for example, in the failure of the nineteenth-century irrigation boom on the Arkansas River, which flows through western Kansas; and it knew the extravagant hopes that had once gathered around towns like Garden City; and it was sure that there would never be enough reservoirs to satisfy the water demand nor any cheap or easy imports available from other regions.[25]

In retrospect the committee underestimated the resourcefulness of the region's people in finding water, and it failed to anticipate the extraordinary change that irrigation would make in the next half-century of plains agriculture. Over the short run at least, technology would indeed make a greater abundance possible where there had been extreme scarcity. But in the long run, the committee was absolutely right: irrigation farming would be doomed to disappointment. Water is still, after many decades of water development, a severely limited resource on the Plains, and it will be even more scarce in the future than it is today. Ironically part of that future scarcity will be due to atmospheric pollution caused by the high-energy technology that has given a passing victory.

The water that was "invented" as a response to the Dust Bowl, a supply that was not well understood or widely appreciated in the 1930s, was the High Plains aquifer, which underlies the region from Texas to South Dakota, and includes as its largest unit the Ogallala Formation. During Miocene time (5 to 24 million years ago) deep beds of sand and gravel were deposited on the Plains by streams flowing down from the Rockies. Today those beds lie buried underground and are saturated with the rainfall of millions of years, accumulating at rates varying from less than 0.1 inch in Texas to 6 inches a year in south-central Kansas. Like the rate of recharge, the thickness of the saturated beds varies considerably; Nebraska and Wyoming have by far the largest share of the water.[26]

Pumping the High Plains aquifer first began on an extensive scale in the Texas panhandle right after World War Two. By 1957 there were over forty thousand pumps there pouring water on the fields. Pumps were working noisily night and day over in New Mexico too, and all the way north to the Sand Hills of Nebraska, pumping water in wet and dry years alike. Some of them burned gasoline, others diesel fuel or natural gas. Though originally touted as an emergency remedy to be used during drought, the irrigation pumps soon became a permanent, everyday form of production, and on them a new way of rural life, very different from that of the old sodbuster and dryland farmer, came to depend. They did much to stabilize the agricultural economy and population. By the late fifties, deep-well irrigation annually contributed more than 20 percent to the region's income—several hundred million dollars a year that meant for many farms and towns the margin between prosperity and bankruptcy. No wonder then, with that miraculous achievement all around them, that the people of the Plains put their faith in technological adaptation more than ever. If nature had laid down those underground deposits of water and fuel, it was man who had discovered and brought them to the surface, turning them into wealth. The mayor of Lubbock, Texas, expressed the common confidence in technological innovation when he declared, "The history of this country is that as the need arose for anything, somebody was there with the right tool to take care of it. This is the way this country was built."[27] The unacknowledged problem in that confidence was that this country was not built to last. Irrigated agriculture was a mode of production that could not be sustained.

In 1978 there were about 170,000 wells punched down into the aquifer, and they were annually withdrawing 23 million acre-feet (enough water to cover 23 million acres one foot deep). The total irrigated acreage amounted that year to 13 million. Though only one in ten acres was irrigated, almost half of the region's crop value came from those acres. The extraordinary crop production allowed by that irrigation supported a vast livestock industry, worth $10 billion a year.[28] In fact the raising and slaughtering of American beef had by 1978 been revolutionized by plains irrigation, as the stockyards of Chicago closed down and the leading packing houses moved west, to be nearer the supply of grain, and as cattle moved off the range and onto feedlots, where they were mass-fed and mass-fattened. All this took a heavy toll on the aquifer. By 1980 Texans had pumped up 114 million acre- feet, Kansans 29 million-feet, which is more water than ten Colorado Rivers could furnish in a year. By the mid-1980s farmers in parts of those states had so depleted the underground supply that they had to go down 300 feet to find the water table. Many pumps had to shut down, and new ones could not be set up.

In every state the depletion of the Ogallala aquifer led to the creation of government agencies to slow the rate of depletion and stretch the supply as far into the future as possible: a state Groundwater Commission and local groundwater-management districts in Colorado, a state Department of Water Resources and local natural-resource districts in Nebraska, and similar institutions in Texas. In state after state, it became standard practice to require government permits for new wells, along with flowmeters in some areas to gauge and control the rate of pumping; rules on minimum well spacing and the like also appeared. However much independent-minded farmers resented these infringements on their prerogatives to do what they liked with their land and the water underlying it, they had little choice but to accept them if they wanted to stay in business. Even then, despite the dramatic political change in their lives, the water tables continued to drop. The regulations only managed to slow the rate of depletion, not achieve an equilibrium state in which recharge balanced withdrawal. The mining continued, and no new source of water lay in sight.[29]

Funded by a multimillion-dollar grant from the federal government, six of the Plains states undertook to study the economic impact of the inevitable decline of their water and energy resources.[30] The study for my own state, published in 1982 by the Kansas Water Office, began by accepting what had been for so long unacceptable: the idea that nature, even the deep underground aquifer of the Plains, is limited and exhaustible. By the year 2020, the study indicated, 75 percent of the irrigated acreage in western Kansas will be lost, or 1.6 million acres. Long before the water is gone, the natural gas to pump it will be gone. Remarkably two economists at Kansas State University concluded that this depletion will have no ill effect on Plains communities; population, they predicted, will increase by 20 percent and total personal income by 130 percent, and that despite the fact that farming on those 1.6 million acres must revert to dryland methods, which involve fallowing half of one's acreage every year (allowing that land to lie idle in order to accumulate soil moisture) and planting wheat and grain sorghum rather than corn. This amazingly rosy-eyed conclusion came out of a Department of Agriculture computer model that projected commodity price increases of 20 to 50 percent for the major dryland crops. In the real world of international markets, however, American farmers have watched their prices *fall*, not increase, due to increasingly intense competition from other producer nations. When and if global warming becomes evident, that competitive situation may be even worse for the Plains. But then the economists ignored completely the possibility of global warming, as they did the lessons of the past, of changing international relations, and of foreign agricultural development. Despite its enormous cost, the study failed to take into account almost all of the critical uncertainties and thus failed to confront the stark, bleak prospect of a Plains that will be forced back to practicing the same nonirrigated, high-risk farming that prevailed prior to the 1930s.[31]

A similar story, with varying terminal dates, could be told for every section of the Great Plains, so that by the time global warming begins to show up in higher summer temperatures and lower rainfall, the irrigation empire will already have nearly collapsed. We will have to face the desiccation without the aid of the Ogallala, without affordable fuel, without the miracle of pipe-and-pump technology. That short-term technological miracle, in other words, by stimulating so much development and investment so fast, may have made the future calamity far worse than it might otherwise have been.[32]

Can another technological miracle be produced and in the nick of time? The ever-popular hope on the Plains is that some agency of government will tap a major river system outside the area and pump in "surplus" water to save the irrigators. The most frequently mentioned sources are the Missouri or Mississippi or Columbia, the Great Lakes, or the northward-flowing rivers of Canada. These are hardly new hopes. Each one has been debated thoroughly and repeatedly, even been put before voters and rejected. A proposed Texas Water Plan, for example, was the subject of a statewide referendum in 1969. It projected spending $3.5 billion to take water from the Mississippi below New Orleans and carry it all the way to the High Plains via a series of canals and reservoirs, covering a distance of twelve hundred miles and a rise in elevation of thirty-six hundred feet. The scheme would have required nearly half the electricity consumed in Texas to pump the water that far and that high. Despite overwhelming support from the political, business, and agricultural establishment, the plan failed to get a majority vote and, unless

Texas suddenly finds itself awash in revenues, seems unlikely to be reconsidered; it is simply too expensive and uneconomical. Residents in the eastern half of the state are not interested in furnishing the money that the western half would need to finance the project, and hardly anyone maintains that it could ever be self-financing.[33] Less populous states, such as Kansas and Nebraska, do not have anywhere near the wherewithal to fund similar projects on their own. Moreover in the unlikely event that they raise sufficient funding, they would have to convince other states to let them do the diverting, and already the barge owners on the lower Missouri, who depend on maintaining high-water levels, are in a state of panic over upstream impoundments and irrigation withdrawals. That leaves the federal government as the only force that could conceivably undertake such expensive, interstate engineering projects—but then one should add that only the American government of another era could have undertaken it, not the deficit-ridden government of today. Even a federal government with unlimited funds might find it economically irrational to invest $330 per acre-foot to develop water, which was the estimated cost for West Texas farmers in 1969, or to invest $2,000 or more per acre-foot, which might very well be the future cost of water on the Plains. What crops could possibly justify so large an investment? There are none. Only if global warming seriously threatened domestic food supplies would the American government be likely to try to fund such capital- intensive water projects.[34]

All those difficulties facing new water-importation schemes, difficulties that have stymied the schemes for more than twenty years, pale beside those that will appear in an era experiencing global warming. Recall that over the central and western region of North America the rains will become scarcer and scarcer, the rivers and lakes fall lower and lower. Surplus water may be as rare as a cloud in June. Consequently irrigation may go into widespread decline in every western state, and the shrinking supply of water could be captured, not by farmers, but by urban consumers in Denver, Albuquerque, Boise, Phoenix, and Los Angeles. Every watershed could become even more fiercely protective of its supply. Already crumbling is the timeworn hope that "someplace else" must have a water surplus that can be diverted to slake thirsty farmers. Only a most extraordinary technological breakthrough—for example, building a string of ocean desalting plants along the Pacific Coast powered by nuclear fusion—could possibly give that hope a new plausibility.

Never mind for the moment all the environmental costs that intensive irrigation has led to, including an altered soil structure, fertilizer and herbicide pollution of groundwater, and the heavy nitrate runoff from cattle feedlots; environmental costs that future generations must pay without enjoying the benefits of the water. Never mind the social costs that this expensive mode of production has entailed, costs that can be seen in increasing farm sizes, declining rural population, and shrinking small towns. Concentrate only on the simple fact, agreed on by almost everybody, that we are beginning to see the end of the irrigation era. That particular technological triumph over nature has about run its course, leaving us once more vulnerable to blowing dust, poverty, and out-migration.[35]

My point is not that technology is an evil or dangerous ally or that new technological solutions should be completely rejected. We will need a spirit of innovation in the future more than ever. One of the most promising ideas on the horizon is the creation, through plant genetics, of a new kind of agriculture that uses well-adapted native plants as the basis of plains farming. The scientist Wes Jackson has called that agriculture a system of "perennial polyculture," for it would involve cultivating and harvesting a mix of perennial grasses, mimicking the complex mosaic that nature displays in a prairie ecosystem. A field converted to that system would stretch before the eye like a prairie of old, offering a diversity of grasses, legumes, and forbs billowing in the wind, and it would need no irrigation, artificial fertilizer, pesticides, or plowing or harrowing, and much less gasoline or propane.[36] Science, Jackson believes, has the capacity to design a far better agriculture than we have yet devised, and he is right. Someday his vision of an ecologically informed agriculture may indeed be the norm on the Plains. But every scientific innovation or technological panacea, it should be clear, has hidden within its promise the disappointment of unforeseen costs and the possibility of unanticipated catastrophe. Depending completely on human intelligence to master a volatile environment is a far more risky strategy than the popular mind realizes, and one more filled with ambiguity and defeat. Science and technology appear to offer an easy way out of our difficulties with nature, but easy ways are usually hard ways to sustain and more hazardous than we have realized.

A third and more hopeful lesson we can draw from history is that the best strategy for avoiding another thirties-style catastrophe lies in restoring more of the Plains to their natural, preagricultural condition. We have a habit, rooted in our economic institutions, of pushing agricultural development too far, beyond what the environment can bear, and now we must overcome that habit and lower our demands on this fragile land, returning much of the country to a more natural state. Probably the only practical way that can be done is either through local zoning of land use, state or federal purchase of title, or some program of conservation easements on those portions of the Great Plains that are the most ecologically vulnerable. Such lands must be identified and permanently taken out of production, out of the marketplace, and out of the reach of private, short-term self-interest.

If early predictions that the entire Great Plains would be forever off limits to agriculture proved false, the opposite view that every single acre might be made to produce food and profit has been equally wrong. Moreover, the latter view has been very expensive. Severe wind erosion has continued to plague the region from time to time, following cycles of plowup and abandonment. Whenever drought has appeared, it has cost American taxpayers billions of dollars in bailout money, and in accepting that money repeatedly, the region has become dependent on the federal government for its survival. This has perhaps been the single most important outcome of the 1930s. A greater panacea than even irrigation, which only brings in water and then for a minority of farmers, the government has brought in cash, lots of cash, pumping it through an elaborate system of pipelines called "farm programs" and spreading that cash over virtually every farm and ranch, in order to keep agriculture alive on the Plains. The most common conclusion drawn from the Dust Bowl experience was "seek federal assistance," and that conclusion has now become a well-entrenched policy. No technological innovation, no local spirit of determination, has produced nearly as much income security as Washington, D.C., has done. But this is also a dependency that has serious flaws, which will become manifest as long-term desiccation sets in.

The federal government has provided massive amounts of assistance, because Americans have been a generous people toward those who take risks and fail. Risk is widely celebrated as a national virtue. In our schools, competitive sports, market economy, government policies, and entertainment, we have constantly encouraged such behavior, believing as we do that by encouraging individual risk we all prosper. That was the assumption directing the land policies of the nation in the nineteenth century, when the Plains were first settled, and the assumption has not altered much in the last decade of the twentieth century. Western mythology still celebrates those men and women who risked all to push the frontier forward, putting family and community behind them as

restraints on enterprise, itching to get out of the older settlements and
their confining ways, going out onto the Plains to acquire property, in
many cases grabbing it illegally and with impunity, then pushing against
its ecological limits to determine what it could yield in the way of wealth.
But a land policy that encourages such risk taking also produces a lot of
failures, people who bet the whole farm and lose all. The Great Plains has
always had, by world standards, a high percentage of high-rolling
gamblers—colorful, brash, self-reliant in rhetoric, dismissive of any
criticism—and again and again they have gone beyond what the land can
bear. Our persistent unwillingness to discourage such behavior, to put
communal and environmental stability ahead of individualistic specula-
tion and acquisitiveness as a social good, has been by far the biggest
obstacle to successful adaptation on the Plains.

Not every plainsdweller in history, of course, has been an overconfi-
dent speculator. Many have been unfortunate, powerless people forced
by the American lottery of land and opportunity to try to extract a living
out here on the fringes of the good earth. Since settlement first began on
the Plains a hundred years ago, many desperate people have come and
gone with the volatile cycles of climate. There are fewer of them now
than before on the land, but some are still there, trying to scrape an
income out of sand dunes or other marginal ground.

One of the major achievements of the 1930s was to extend the
protective hand of the federal government, indiscriminately and liberally, to both the foolhardy risk takers and the helpless victims, and indeed
to the whole spectrum of farm operators, whenever they suffer from the
chaotic climate of drought and winds. I have mentioned the Works
Progress Administration handing out help in the Depression, but there
have been many other, and more permanent, forms of agricultural
assistance, which either began in the thirties or have appeared since
then, including not only all the well-known programs to support farm-
commodity prices, but also what has become a regularized, permanent
system of disaster assistance.

Even before the Dust Bowl period, state and federal agencies extended
loans to farmers to replace the seed and feed they lost to drought. In 1934
the New Deal's Federal Emergency Relief Administration took over that
role, then gave way to the WPA. Other relief came from farm-loan banks
to lift the burden of debt, higher tariffs to keep out international
competitors, the Agricultural Adjustment Administration and its suc-
cessor, the Soil Conservation and Domestic Allotment Program, the
Federal Surplus Relief Corporation (which later became the Federal

Surplus Commodities Corporation). One estimate puts the total cost of all federal programs for the Plains from 1933 to 1939 at less than $1 billion, but that figure leaves out the nonfarm aid that flowed into the region during those years, bringing many indirect benefits to farmers. Whatever the full expense, it was the New Deal's welfare philosophy that saved many rural communities from utter rout. Eventually such public benevolence became public duty, demanded year in and year out, whenever there was a state of emergency. By the droughty years of 1953–56, Washington officials were *expected* to rush aid to whoever had gotten in trouble trying to farm the Plains, and they dared not say no. They pumped in surplus food to feed people, surplus grains to feed livestock, and emergency credit and loans to sustain farm operations. During the single crop year of 1977–78, when serious drought struck again, the bureaucrats spent almost $1 billion on a relief package, plus extending indirect aid through such offices as the Farmers Home Administration, the Small Business Administration, and the Federal Crop Insurance Corporation.[37]

Each new drought since the thirties has seen the level of relief, and the bureaucracy that administers it, increase exponentially.[38] In the most recent dry spell of 1988, severe but short-lived and centered mainly on the Dakotas, the government sent out a whopping $4 billion in relief money. All of that sum was supposed to go to alleviate drought conditions, but Associated Press reporters uncovered massive fraud around the country; some farmers collected cash payments of hundreds of thousands of dollars for damages from wind, rain, hail, frost, fungus, insects, "anything related to nature," as one county administrator explained.[39]

Farming, we are frequently told in the farm journals and government publications, must be a business like any other; but that is not quite the way things have developed. Farming is instead a business that passes many of its risks on to taxpayers. Great Plains farmers are unique only in the great extent of their dependency: they regularly pursue a business that relies on people in other regions of the country to step in and save them from bankruptcy whenever nature, or their own miscalculation, threatens. They have managed to shift a critical part of their burden to the anonymous taxpaying public—to millions of total strangers who have agreed to cushion them from a hard world.

What has been the ecological effect of so much kindness? Has it lessened the pressure to adapt agriculture to local conditions? Has it saved farmers from the disciplining hand of natural forces, even encouraged them to try to push their land to the breaking point? Removing risk from the marketplace, we are told by many economists, results in inefficiency and waste, though for many good reasons the government does so anyway. What happens when we remove risk from the physical environment? Does it lead to an overextension of agriculture that cannot be sustained? I think it does.

That conclusion is not one that some scholars of natural hazards would draw. Like floods and other calamities, they argue, droughts are an evil visited on innocent humankind by nature, and the best remedy is to develop a complex, risk-spreading system that can alleviate the pain and suffering they cause. According to this view, precisely such a system has emerged since the thirties in the form of a responsive federal government. We now live, it is said, in a "mature" society, with a central authority that is well organized to give assistance in time of need. Tracking the history of distress indices on the Plains, these scholars note a lessening of bankruptcy, out-migration, and social instability over time. In the 1890s crisis, when laissez-faire was the national philosophy, millions had to abandon the region simply to avoid starvation. During the drought of the 1970s, however, hardly anyone had to leave because of ecological conditions. The next severe drought, according to this view, will have even less of an impact than the last one, due to the continuing integration of the American economy and the growth of organized disaster management. This organization of risk, they say, is how modern complex societies learn to adapt to nature; they concentrate enough power and wealth at the center in order to overcome most natural vicissitudes.[40]

That has indeed been one of the most important strategies followed over the past half century, but it may be a poor one to rely on as global warming appears. Desiccation is a long-term process, lasting for perhaps a century or more. Calling on other areas of the nation to share their income with the Plains over that period of time may be unrealistic; and as those regions encounter their own climate-related difficulties, it may be like expecting other western watersheds to release some of their precious water. They may have little money to release, and they may even reject the idea of their taxes going to support an agriculture where it seems marginal, uneconomic, and irrational. Helping the Plains through an occasional hazardous period is one thing, but helping support them decade after decade in an effort to defy the forces of nature is another. Instead of continuing to function as a compensatory, risk-spreading force, the government, reflecting its own straitened circumstances, might begin to insist that the Plains rely on themselves to adapt and survive.

The notion that a complex, highly integrated, and centralized society

will be always ready to meet the threat of a future Dust Bowl is itself open
to question. If one examines the long historical record of social adaptation to nature, complex societies seem to be more vulnerable than simple
ones. Despite their well-developed administrative structure and their
capacity to call on vast pools of labor and resources, such societies may
be quite vulnerable to long-term environmental adversity and may
collapse or withdraw instead of adapting. They commonly lack a detailed, intimate understanding of the many local environments on which
they depend or which they exploit. They substitute money for that
knowledge. They find it hard to make fundamental changes of direction.
They grow discouraged and fall apart. That conclusion emerged from
discussions among a number of anthropologists at a Canadian conference on how modern civilization might cope with rapid climate change.
The report of that conference argued:

> The idea that complex societies—modern technological societies
> included—are *more* vulnerable to climate change than less complex
> societies will undoubtedly come as an unwelcome surprise to many
> people. The rapid pace of technological development in the
> industrialized nations since the second world war has created the
> comfortable illusion of increasing human *invulnerability* to the vagaries
> of nature. This illusion is not only wrong but dangerous. There's every
> reason to believe the complex nature of modern societies renders them
> more susceptible to internal collapse than hunter-gatherer or agriculture
> societies of the past, or even those groups which today preserve hunter-
> gatherer or subsistence agricultural roots—for example, native
> populations of the Canadian North and traditional agricultural groups
> such as the Amish or the Pueblos.[41]

Admittedly these authors have in mind a catastrophe like nuclear
winter, a global cooling caused by the detonation of the world's nuclear
arsenal, which would leave most urban Americans in a state of helpless
hunger, completely unable to get enough food as the whole elaborate
agribusiness system collapsed. But even in the less sudden, less cataclys-
mic scenario of global warming, much of the apparatus of the so-called
"mature" society might break down, stressed beyond its ability to cope or
beyond its political will to do so. And in that collapse of central support,
the Plains might be left worse off than ever: weak on adaptive skills, too
long complacent about their "triumph" to take nature seriously, so
tightly integrated into the national and international economy that they
would not have, say, the Eskimo's flexibility in a crisis.

However unreliable it may prove to be, the federal government will undoubtedly be called on to help with the process of adapting agriculture to the future Plains. Whether ecologically wisely or not, we have reached the point of expecting government to be active in such situations. What then should its aims be? What would be its best role? What strategy does the history of the region suggest that government might promote to achieve the best possible adaptation for the longest time and under the greatest adversity? Where does the public interest lie—in supporting overextended farm acreage and production at the cost of ecological degradation, or in reducing that acreage and production to fit the best-estimate, long-term limits of the land? I believe the clear answer is the latter.

Altogether the Great Plains states of the United States and Canada contain about 800 million acres. Few of those acres have been permanently put off limits to row-crop agriculture. A few parks and wildlife refuges, a series of national grasslands that do not exceed 1 percent of the total—and that is all we have designated by law for perpetual protection. The rest is in private hands, and we leave it largely up to the marketplace to determine how that land should be used. If the world price of wheat goes up, the plow gets to work turning grassland into wheatland. If the price goes down, the land reverts to some form of cover, weeds or grass, and may for a while support a herd of cattle. Whatever the decision, it is for the most part private landowners who make it, and they decide according to the principle of self-interest, rational or not, in response to a world market economy.

In recent years, to be sure, the government has tried to become a more active counterforce to that market economy and has tried repeatedly to set aside land for nonproductive purposes. In so doing it has acknowledged that entrepreneurial risk taking needs to be counterbalanced by collective measures. The Soil Bank program of the 1950s, for example, idled over 21 million acres across the nation, though its purpose was to reduce crop surpluses rather than to protect vulnerable soils. During the 1970s international grain markets boomed, thanks in part to Soviet purchases, and for the first time in decades, the government encouraged farmers to increase production, even if it meant plowing from "fence row to fence row." Following that advice, they plowed up millions of fragile rangeland and other highly erodible land; nationally the great plow-up of the seventies added 56 million acres to production.[42]

Later even free-market enthusiasts began to question the wisdom of this new round of unrestrained expansion, and during the Reagan presidency a movement gathered support from both conservatives and

liberals to set up controls over "sodbusting" and "swampbusting" (draining wetlands to plant crops). The Conservation Reserve Program was the
outcome, established under the Food Security Act of 1985 to help adjust
agriculture to its environmental conditions, by renting some of the most
marginal lands—up to a maximum of 25 percent of the area in any single
county—and putting it back into grass, keeping it there for a period of ten
years. The average rental across the region costs the government about
$50 an acre per year, or $500 an acre over the duration of the program,
which means that the government is paying the farmer more in rental
fees than most Great Plains land costs to buy. The goal of the CRP is
eventually to retire 45 million acres from production, about half of that
on the Great Plains; but the program is temporary, and all those acres
could revert to cropping when the program expires. Renewing the
program is a possibility, but the CRP is also a very expensive kind of
remedy. Should we go on paying such high rents to farmers into the next
century and continue such a strategy to meet the potential desiccation?
That could be the most expensive program the Department of Agriculture has ever embarked on, and even then it would always be a stop-gap
measure. As Earle J. Bedenbaugh, deputy administrator of the USDA's
Agricultural Stabilization and Conservation Service, has admitted, we
have been making "short-term solutions to long-term problems," and "at
some point in time we are going to have to take a basic sound philosophy
concerning agricultural legislation, put it into effect, and see it to its
ultimate end."[43]

What should that permanent philosophy be? Looking at the long
history of plains settlement, the historian concludes that only a program
of permanent grassland restoration has any economic or ecological
rationality to it. We need to put a larger part of the burden of adaptation
on nature, which has been at that sort of work for hundreds of millions
of years. Such a program could only be carried out by collective means,
either through local zoning or federal purchase of land, or the purchase
of conservation easements in perpetuity, in order to control all future
development of that land.

Almost all federal programs to date, excepting the small, submarginal
purchase program in the thirties, which transferred to public ownership
about 12 million acres across the West, have been based on the sanctity
of private property. The ultimate power to dispose of the Great Plains
has remained with the private individual, who decides whether to rent
the land to the government or not. That decision will almost always be
based on the principle of maximizing personal gain; so landowners have

been taught to calculate, and so they act in most cases. Despite all those federal programs for relief and assistance, despite decades of conservation programs to adapt farming practices, we have not in this fundamental respect come very far since the 1930s—or for that matter, since the 1880s.

Is so much reliance on private self-interest the way to achieve the best possible adaptation to the climate, either the climate of the past or the climate of the future? In the midst of every drought, knowledgeable observers have answered "no" and called for changing that pattern of land use by changing the pattern of landownership to some substantial degree. They have estimated that several million acres—the estimates vary considerably, though some fifty to one hundred million acres, or two to four times the acreage in the CRP program, would be a rough consensus—ought to be retired permanently from all crop use and restored to something like their presettlement vegetation.

The most recent proposal along these lines comes from two land-use planners, Frank and Deborah Popper, of Rutgers University, who have stirred up a storm of outrage among western people. In 1987 they began arguing, with some hyperbole, that farming on the Great Plains has been "a 100-year-old mistake," a charge that ignored the fact that over much of that period the Plains have produced an enormous pile of food and money, and thus can boast some success as well as failure. Later the Poppers moderated their charge by examining the specific areas of the Plains that have been most vulnerable. Using 1990 census data, they have demonstrated that the region is once more going through a cycle of economic stress and shrinkage, forcing us to acknowledge that a large part of the Plains is agriculturally marginal and ought to be retired from crop production. They have advocated a program of ecological restoration, called the "Buffalo Commons," in which native animals would return to roam over a vast federally owned grassland. The vision of bison returning to the landscape, of the landscape returning to a state of quasi nature, is outrageous to many residents who have devoted their lives to the conquest of nature; that outcome would represent nothing less than a defeat. But as the Poppers point out with stark demographic data, much of the Plains is already losing people and cannot survive without outside financial aid—a calamity that is occurring even before any climate warming has begun. A program of grassland restoration in areas of greatest environmental and economic vulnerability, combined with new, nonagricultural uses of the land, such as tourism, appears to be the only practical remedy.[44]

The exact distribution of those fifty to one hundred million acres to be restored can be determined only by ecologists and soil scientists, working with knowledgeable local residents. However brought under protection, they should be in large enough blocs to allow effective management. They should be restored in a manner that would minimize any adverse effect on rural communities. In some cases the restored lands might be used for livestock grazing, whether cattle or bison, but gingerly and only under close supervision. They should be restored to a diverse set of organisms, reconstituting native ecosystems as fully as science can manage, and they should form interconnected corridors, through which those plants and animals can migrate northward as the warming begins. Their preservation should be the responsibility not only of the federal government but also of the local residents, who must, for the sake of their own survival, learn to practice a stewardship of the nonproductive as well as the productive resources.

The private landowner cannot or will not undertake such a program of market withdrawal and ecological restoration. He or she will never find a large enough market in tourism or whatever alternative uses there may be to make such a program profitable or attractive. Only some disinterested group of individuals, acting in the public interest, or some government agency, whether federal, state, or local, could ever under-take it. They would do so not because they were more intelligent than the private owner, but because they would have more freedom to ignore the abrupt swings of market economics.

In my view, the most compelling lesson we can learn from the history of the Great Plains is that the best adaptation to climate can never be achieved merely by private-property institutions or entrepreneurial thinking. Nor can it be achieved by merely establishing a generous program of government relief, compensating operators for losses from drought. The appeal of our present system of chasing global markets while passing risks on to other regions lies in the impressive quantity of wealth it produces and in the political popularity of its subsidies. It does not really lie in its environmental flexibility nor its capacity for accom-modation to nature. To insist otherwise would be to turn the ideas of private ownership and free enterprise into an economic fundamentalism that ignores all historical experience and is immune to critical thinking.

In drawing this conclusion from the past, I have not really addressed the critical question of how the threat of global warming might be prevented or lessened at its source—the tailpipes and smokestacks of the greater industrial world. Obviously any comprehensive solution to the region's vulnerability must lie in curtailing the pollution of the earth's atmosphere with carbon, a solution beyond the power of plains residents to carry out alone. What they can do, however, in cooperation with public officials, is to examine their history critically and ask what it suggests as their best regional strategy for mitigating the social and ecological effects of global change.

The challenge of cultural adaptation to environment, contrary to the opinion of some technological and scientific experts, has never been easy to meet anywhere in the world. It has been harder on the Plains than in most regions. For more than a hundred years now, men and women have been out here working hard at the task of farming, and they still have not really figured out how to meet the basic challenge of the land for very long. We have settled the landscape with farms and towns, but then watched many of those settlements dwindle away; more such decline lies ahead. We have made a great deal of money out of the land, but in recent years more farm income has come from government sources, less from the marketplace. And for every generation, there has been the threat of blowing dust and ravaged crops. If we have not solved the riddle of the country so far, how can we expect to solve it easily in the future, in those remorseless, unclouded summers that may lie ahead?

The future of the American West, like its past, may hold profound lessons about the vulnerability of our achievement. A century ago the Plains were boom country, leading the whole western region in population and economic growth. Even today, when the main growth has shifted toward the urban Sunbelt, the Plains remain an important repository of western cultural identity. Here is where so much of our regional memory has been forged. Whole communities of wild animals have come and gone, whole nations of Indian peoples have risen and fallen, along with a succession of cowboys and cowtowns, homesteaders and modern farmers. Expunge them all from memory, wipe out their traces on the land, as we have done again and again, and you wipe out much of what the West has meant to the nation and the world. For many reasons, the specter of global warming being only one of them, that process of wiping out our past is looming before us.

The entire American West is rapidly expunging its traditions, as it is changing its landscape. The rural communities that have meant so much to the region's identity may soon go the way of the buffalo herds and traditional Indian tribal life. Even the desert metropolises, now so triumphant, may be more insecure than we realize, if their supplies of water and energy continue to decline. This process of change is, of course, inevitable to a point. Environmental history does not reveal a steady course of westward expansion or of secular progress, but rather a pattern of erratic cycles that go back as far as we can look, into the ancient history of rocks and tectonic forces. Nowhere in the West have we any reason to think we have escaped that pattern of nature, or even escaped the cycles of boom and bust created by our own deeds and mistakes. We have not mastered the place nor built a secure civilization with its raw materials. We have not even understood it very well.

Notes

Chapter 1

1. The earliest biographical sketch was by M. D. Lincoln, "John Wesley Powell," *The Open Court* 16 (December 1902): 705–15. For later biographies see notes 26–28. I have also profited from reading James Aton's "Inventing John Wesley Powell: The Major, His Admirers and Cash-Register Dams in the Colorado River Basin," Distinguished Faculty Lecture No. 9, Southern Utah State College, December 1, 1988.

2. John C. Frémont, *The Exploring Expedition to the Rocky Mountains in the Year 1842* (1945; Washington, D.C.: Smithsonian Institution Press, 1988), 131.

3. A far more distinguished scholarly work than that popular literature is William Goeztmann's *Exploration and Empire: The Explorer and the Scientist in the Winning of the West* (New York: Knopf, 1966), chapter 15. In his title, however, and in his treatment of Powell as the last in a line of imperialists, Goetzmann echoes much of that popular romantic thinking.

4. See, for instance, William E. Warne's *The Bureau of Reclamation* (New York: Praeger, 1973), 4: "Students of reclamation consider Major Powell the father of irrigation development.... [T]he mark of that great conservationist of the nineteenth century was indelibly imprinted on the Reclamation Service." The lineage supposedly runs from the U.S. Geological Survey, of which Powell was the second and most influential director, to a wide array of other government bureaus. See W. C. Mendenhall, "The United States Geological Survey," *Scientific Monthly* 36 (February 1933):117.

5. John Wesley Powell, *Exploration of the Colorado River and Its Canyons* (*Exploration of the Colorado River of the West and Its Tributaries*, 1875; New York: Penguin Books, 1987), 98.

6. John Wesley Powell, *Report on the Lands of the Arid Region* (Washington,

D.C.: Government Printing Office, 1878), 1. This book, according to Samuel Trask Dana and Sally K. Fairfax in *Forest and Range Policy: Its Development in the United States* (New York: McGraw-Hill Book Co., 1980, 2nd ed), 39, "contends with [George Perkins] Marsh's work for the distinction of being the most significant document in American conservation history."

7. Powell, *Report on the Lands of the Arid Region*, 46–56. Shott's data showed a range of from 15 inches to nearly 28 inches in the subhumid region, of from 4 inches (at Yuma, Arizona) to 20 inches in the arid region, and of from 16 inches to nearly 80 inches in the region of the lower Columbia River.

8. Powell, *Report on the Lands of the Arid Region*, 41.

9. Select Committee on Irrigation of Arid Lands, *Ceding the Arid Lands to the States and Territories*, 51st Congress, 2d sess., House Report No. 3767 (Washington, D.C.: Government Printing Office, 1891), 12–13, 24–37, 71–139, 172–84.

10. Select Committee on Irrigation, 84.

11. Select Committee on Irrigation, 133–34.

12. Population statistics come from U.S. Census Office, *Report on Population of the United States at the Eleventh Census: 1890, Part I* (Washington, D.C.: Government Printing Office, 1895). The only other cities in the seventeen-state area that had more than twenty thousand people were Galveston, Houston, Dallas, Kansas City, and Omaha. In that year Phoenix had barely three thousand inhabitants, and Albuquerque had less than six thousand (combining both its old and new towns).

13. Thomas G. Alexander criticizes Powell's commonwealth idea as being "highly impractical," because it required far more of a consensus about economic development than existed in the West. See his "The Powell Irrigation Survey and the People of the Mountain West," *Journal of the West* 7 (January 1968):52.

14. Daniel Coit Gilman, "In Memory of John Wesley Powell," *Science* 16 (14 November 1902):784; Alexander Chamberlain, "In Memoriam: John Wesley Powell," *Journal of American Folk Lore* 16 (July/September 1902):202; William Healey Dall, "John Wesley Powell," *Bulletin of the Philosophical Society of Washington* 14 (1900–1904):308; Gilbert H. Grosvenor, "John Wesley Powell," *National Geographic Magazine* 13 (November 1902):393; William Brewer, "John Wesley Powell," *American Journal of Science* 14 (1902):382.

15. William M. Davis, "John Wesley Powell," *National Academy of Sciences: Biographical Memoirs* 8 (Washington, D.C.: National Academy of Sciences, 1919), 45–46. Davis was the second director of the Reclamation Service. William Herbert Hobbs, "John Wesley Powell, 1834–1902," *Scientific Monthly* 39 (December 1934):528; Grove Karl Gilbert, "John Wesley Powell," *Science* 16 (10 Oct. 1902):566. The latter's relationship to Powell is described in Stephen J. Pyne's *Grove Karl Gilbert: A Great Engine of Research* (Austin: University of Texas Press, 1980), 77–79.

16. At the time Roosevelt took office, there were 45 million acres of national forest reserves; in his two terms he added nearly 150 million more acres, all in the West.

17. Theodore Roosevelt, *An Autobiography* (New York: Macmillan, 1916), 408–36. In his sole mention of Powell, Roosevelt lauds him for his early leadership in western irrigation development, but then dismisses him for failing to see "the need for saving the forests and the soil" (p. 8). That was a distortion of Powell's position; he opposed a strong *federal* role in conservation. For background on Roosevelt's conservation thought, see G. Edward White, *The Eastern Establishment and the Western Experience: The West of Frederic Remington, Theodore Roosevelt, and Owen Wister* (New Haven: Yale University Press, 1968), chapter 8.

18. *Report of the National Conservation Commission*, 60th Cong., 2d sess., Senate Document 676 (Washington, D.C.: Government Printing Office, 1909), 3, 124. Pinchot's own definition of conservation was "the application of common sense to the common problems for the common good" (p. 123).

19. Herbert Croly, *The Promise of American Life* (1909; Cambridge, Mass.: Harvard University Press, 1965). The editor of this reprint, Arthur M. Schlesinger, Jr., writes that "what Croly did was to give the views of Theodore Roosevelt an extended historical and sociological setting," though Croly did not echo Roosevelt's emphasis on the conservation of natural resources. In 1914 Croly became the first editor of *The New Republic* magazine.

20. George E. Mowry, *The Era of Theodore Roosevelt and the Birth of Modern America, 1900–1912* (New York: Harper Torchbooks, 1958), 88.

21. Samuel P. Hays, *Conservation and the Gospel of Efficiency: The Progressive Conservation Movement, 1890–1920* (Cambridge, Mass.: Harvard University Press, 1959), 2–3.

22. Walter Prescott Webb, *The Great Plains* (Boston: Ginn, 1931), 2, 419–22. According to Gregory M. Tobin, *The Making of a History: Walter Prescott Webb and "The Great Plains"* (Austin: University of Texas Press, 1976), Webb at one point wanted to write a biography of Powell (p. 113). See also Necah Furman, *Walter Prescott Webb: His Life and Impact* (Albuquerque: University of New Mexico Press, 1976), 105.

23. Senate Committee on Public Lands and Surveys, *To Provide for the Orderly Use, Improvement, and Development of the Public Range*, 73d Cong., 2d sess. (Washington, D.C.: Government Printing Office, 1934), 24, 29. See also E. Louise Peffer, *The Closing of the Public Domain: Disposal and Reservation Policies, 1900–1950* (Stanford: Stanford University Press, 1951), chapters 12–13.

24. Howard, *Montana: High, Wide, and Handsome* (1943; Lincoln: University of Nebraska Press, 1959), 31–34.

25. Henry Nash Smith, *Virgin Land: The American West as Symbol and Myth* (1950; Cambridge, Mass.: Harvard University Press, 1970), 200.

26. William Culp Darrah, *Powell of the Colorado* (Princeton: Princeton University Press, 1951).

27. Paul Meadows, *John Wesley Powell: Frontiersman of Science*. University of Nebraska Studies, New Series No. 10 (July 1952), vii, 60.

28. Wallace Stegner, *Beyond the Hundredth Meridian: John Wesley Powell and the Second Opening of the West* (Boston: Houghton Mifflin, 1954), 361. For DeVoto's critique of American historians' neglect of the West and Powell, see pp. xv–xxiii.

29. Stegner, *Beyond the Hundredth Meridian*, 357. Stegner acknowledged that Powell might see a few dangers in federal stewardship. "He might see, as many conservationists believe they see, a considerable empire-building tendency within the Bureau of Reclamation, an engineer's vision of the West instead of a humanitarian's, a will to build dams without due regard to all the conflicting interests involved. . . . He might join the Sierra Club and other conservation groups in deploring some proposed and 'feasible' dams such as that in Echo Park below the mouth of the Yampa [Utah] . . . " (p. 361). In later years Stegner would intensify his criticism of the federal land and water agencies, but in 1954 he was still, with growing reservations, their supporter against private interests.

30. U. S. Bureau of Census, *State and Metropolitan Area Data Book, 1991* (Washington, D.C.: Government Printing Office, 1992), 202–3. The figure of 79 million is based on the Census of 1990 and is an aggregation of the population of the seventeen westernmost states, excluding Alaska and Hawaii. The largest state is California, with 29.8 million, followed by Texas (17.0), Washington (4.9), Arizona (3.7), and Colorado (3.3).

31. The figures come from U.S. Dept. of Interior, Bureau of Land Management, *Public Land Statistics 1990*, vol. 175 (Washington: Government Printing Office, 1991), 5.

Chapter 2

1. Jean-Pierre Goubert, *The Conquest of Water: The Advent of Health in the Industrial Age*, trans. by Andrew Wilson (Princeton: Princeton University Press, 1989), 51–52. For an account of present-day France's managed water system see Jeremy Purseglove, "Liberty, Ecology, Modernity," *New Scientist* 131 (September 1991):45–48; and the same author's *Taming the Flood* (Oxford: Oxford University Press, 1989).

2. Daniel R. Headrick, *The Tools of Empire: Technology and European Imperialism in the Nineteenth Century* (New York: Oxford University Press, 1981), 11, 210.

3. Quoted in Daniel R. Headrick, *The Tentacles of Progress: Technology Transfer in the Age of Imperialism, 1850–1940* (New York: Oxford University Press, 1988), 171. The literature on British water imperialism in India includes: Ian Stone, *Canal Irrigation in British India: Perspectives on Technological Change in a Peasant Economy* (Cambridge: Cambridge University Press, 1984); Elizabeth Whitcombe, *Agrarian Conditions in Northern India, I: The United Provinces under British Rule, 1860–1900* (Berkeley: University of California Press, 1972); Imran

Ali, *The Punjab under Imperialism, 1885–1947* (Princeton: Princeton University Press, 1988); L. C. A. Knowles, *The Economic Development of the British Overseas Empire*, 2d ed. (London: George Routledge and Sons, 1928), 1:366–83; and among first-hand accounts, Robert Burton Buckley, *The Irrigation Works of India*, 2d ed. (London: E. and F. N. Spon, 1905); and Sir Hanbury Brown, "Irrigation under British Engineers," *Transactions of the American Society of Civil Engineers* 54 C (1905):3–31. For background I have found useful the volume of essays edited by John M. MacKenzie, *Imperialism and the Natural World* (Manchester: Manchester University Press, 1990).

4. B. S. Alexander, George H. Mendell, and George Davidson, *Report of the Board of Commissioners on Irrigation of the San Joaquin, Tulare, and Sacramento Valleys of the State of California* (Washington, D.C.: Government Printing Office, 1874), 42. Davidson, a scientist in the employ of the U.S. Coast Survey, was the principal author of the work. I have discussed him and other American disciples of Indian irrigation in my book *Rivers of Empire: Water, Aridity, and the Growth of the American West* (New York: Oxford University Press, 1985), 143–56.

5. One of the most peripatetic of these engineers was Sir William Willcocks, born in India but removing to Egypt in his early thirties to modernize the Nile. Willcocks toured South Africa, Italy, Canada, and the United States during his long career. A staunch Christian, he defined "the white man's burden" in biblical terms, as one of "replenishing the earth and subduing it." See his autobiography, *Sixty Years in the East* (Edinburgh: William Blackwood, 1935), 72–73.

6. Alfred Deakin, *Irrigated India* (London: W. Thacker, 1893), 285. He was referring to the privately financed Orissa irrigation project, southwest of Calcutta, which went bankrupt.

7. Alexander et al., *Report of the Board of Commissioners*, 57.

8. See Linda J. Lear, "Boulder Dam: A Crossroads in Natural Resource Policy," *Journal of the West* 24 (October 1985):82–94; Joseph E. Stevens, *Hoover Dam: An American Adventure* (Norman: University of Oklahoma Press, 1988); and my own, "Hoover Dam: A Study in Domination," in *Under Western Skies: Nature and History in the American West* (New York: Oxford University Press, 1992), 64–78.

9. Deakin, *Irrigated India,* 146–47.

10. F. Lee Brown and Helen Ingram, *Water and Poverty in the Southwest* (Tucson: University of Arizona Press, 1987), 3. They refer specifically to Hispanos in northern New Mexico and southern Colorado and to American Indians like the Navajo and the Tohono O'odham Nation (also known as the Papago). See also Charles Bowden, *Killing the Hidden Waters* (Austin: University of Texas Press, 1977), part 1.

11. Stanley Crawford, *Mayordomo: Chronicle of an Acequia in Northern New Mexico* (Albuquerque: University of New Mexico, 1988), 176–77. See also Michael C. Meyer, *Water in the Hispanic Southwest: A Social and Legal History,*

1550–1850 (Tucson: University of Arizona Press, 1984). Meyer concludes: "While the native American populations of the desert viewed the precious liquid as the medium of life, the [Spanish] conquerors, missionaries, and settlers viewed it as an instrument of control, a source of power, and most importantly as the fount of accumulated wealth" (p. 167).

12. Deakin, *Irrigated India*, 147–48.

13. A critical study of one key part of the water alliance is Doris Ostrander Dawdy's *Congress in Its Wisdom: The Bureau of Reclamation and the Public Interest* (Boulder, Colo.: Westview Press, 1989).

14. John McPhee, *Encounters with the Archdruid* (New York: Farrar, Straus and Giroux, 1971), part 3. According to McPhee, "The conservation movement is a mystical and religious force, and possibly the reaction to dams is so violent because rivers are the ultimate metaphors of existence, and dams destroy rivers. Humiliating nature, a dam is evil—placed and solid" (p. 140).

15. Norris Hundley's first book was a study of international negotiations over the Colorado River, entitled *Dividing the Waters: A Century of Controversy between the United States and Mexico* (Berkeley: University of California Press, 1966). But it was his second book, *Water and the West: The Colorado River Compact and the Politics of Water in the American West* (Berkeley: University of California Press, 1975), that really situated the subject of water at the center of western development. Though I disagree with some of his interpretations, I highly commend his pioneering work, which has been careful in its research and open and generous in its spirit.

16. Other academic historians who have recently written on the western water supply, water law, or water projects include: Robert Dunbar, Donald Green, Abraham Hoffmann, William Kahrl, Robert Kelley, Lawrence Lee, Donald Pisani, James Sherow, Joseph Stevens, and Daniel Tyler. Among environmental journalists Philip Fradkin and Marc Reisner have been the most prominent.

17. Norris Hundley, Jr., *The Great Thirst: Californians and Water, 1770s–1990s* (Berkeley: University of California Press, 1992).

18. See *Rivers of Empire*, passim.

19. See chapter 1 for a discussion of Progressive Republicanism and Crolyism. The leading proponent of Crolyism, which derives from Alexander Hamilton and Whig-Republicanism, among the western water historians is Robert Kelley, author of *Battling the Inland Sea: American Political Culture, Public Policy, and the Sacramento Valley, 1850–1986* (Berkeley: University of California, 1989).

20. Michael W. Straus, *Why Not Survive?* (New York: Simon and Schuster, 1955), 78. Straus himself did not survive a change in presidential administration; by the time he wrote those words, he had been removed from office by Dwight Eisenhower. Despite his departure and some minor cuts in the reclamation budget, the federal government went on generously funding western water projects until the late 1970s. Even now it is still subsidizing a few new dams and other water-control structures in the West, although the days of the grandiose

projects are over, in part because there are almost no promising sites that have not been developed.

21. Gustavo Esteva, "Development," in *The Development Dictionary: A Guide to Knowledge and Power*, ed. by Wolfgang Sachs (London: Zed Books, 1992), 6–7.

22. See Enar Eskillson, "African Rivers Hold Promise of Major Energy Supply," *Energy International* 15 (July 1978):19–21; K. V. Krishnamurthy, "The Challenge of Africa's Water Development," *Natural Resources Forum* 1 (1977): 369–75; Robert O. Collins, *The Waters of the Nile: Hydropolitics and the Jonglei Canal, 1900–1988* (Oxford: Clarendon Press, 1990), 402–5; Hussein M. Fahim, *Dams, People and Development: The Aswan High Dam Case* (New York: Pergamon Press, 1981); and Neville Rubin and William Warren, eds., *Dams in Africa: An Interdisciplinary Study of Man-Made Lakes in Africa* (London: Frank Cass, 1968).

23. Kevin Kimmage, "Small-scale Irrigation Initiatives in Nigeria: The Problems of Equity and Sustainability," *Applied Geography* 11 (1991): 5; Jan Moris, "Irrigation as a Privileged Solution in African Development," *Development Policy Review* 5 (1987):113; Fred Pearce, "Africa at a Watershed," New Scientist 129 (23 March 1991), 40. See also Thayer Scudder, "River Basin Projects in Africa," *Environment* 31 (March 1989): 4–9, 27–32; Rowena Lawson, "The Volta Resettlement Scheme," *African Affairs* 67 (1968):124–29; and Bjorn Beckman, "Bakolori: The Menace of a Dam," *Development: Seeds of Change* (1985, no. 3):2–32.

24. Vandana Shiva, *Staying Alive: Women, Ecology and Development* (London: Zed Books, 1988), 185. See also her *Ecology and the Politics of Survival: Conflicts over Natural Resources in India* (New Delhi: Sage/United Nations Press, 1991), part 2, which deals extensively with water issues. Another prominent critic is Ramachandra Guha; see his and Madhav Gadgil's *This Fissured Land: An Ecological History of India* (Delhi: Oxford University Press, 1992), chapter 8. For recent discussions of controversial projects, see: N. D. Jayal, "Destruction of Water Resources—The Most Critical Ecological Crisis of East Asia," *Ambio* 14 (1985):95–98; Fred Pearce, "A Dammed Fine Mess," *New Scientist* 130 (4 May 1991):36–39; Omar Sattaur, "Greens in Muddy Water over Indian Dam," *ibid.*, 132 (5 October 1991):16–17; Claude Alvares and Ramesh Billorey, "Damming the Narmada: The Politics behind the Destruction," *The Ecologist* 17 (March/ June 1987):62–73.

25. The most comprehensive critique of water projects is Edward Goldsmith and Nicholas Hildyard's *The Social and Environmental Effects of Large Dams, I: Overview* (Camelford, U.K.: Wadebridge Ecological Centre, 1984). In part 5, "Traditional Irrigation: Learning from the Past," the authors suggest an alternative strategy based on folk culture. See also *II: Case Studies* (1986), which presents thirty-one authors writing on dams in the northern hemisphere, Africa, India, and other Asian countries.

26. I take these figures from World Resources Institute, *World Resources 1988–89* (New York: Basic Books, 1988), chapters 3 and 8.

Chapter 3

1. *Black Elk Speaks, Being the Life Story of a Holy Man of the Oglala Sioux* (1932; Lincoln: University of Nebraska Press, 1961), 9.

2. Hiram Martin Chittenden, *The American Fur Trade of the Far West* (1902; Lincoln: University of Nebraska Press, 1986) 2:807–11, 818. Bernard DeVoto does note that white trappers, like the Indians, looked on the beaver as "very wise—and their job was to outthink him"; *Across the Wide Missouri* (Boston: Houghton Mifflin, 1947), 156. A more thorough account of the beaver's life and ecology appears in David J. Wishart, *The Fur Trade of the American West, 1807–1840: A Geographical Synthesis* (Lincoln: University of Nebraska Press, 1979), 27–33. See also James O'Brien, "The History of North America from the Standpoint of the Beaver," *Free Spirits* 1 (1982): 45–54.

3. Ernest Staples Osgood, *The Day of the Cattleman* (Minneapolis: University of Minnesota Press, 1929); Paul I. Wellman, *The Trampling Herd: The Story of the Cattle Range in America* (Philadelphia: J. B. Lippincott, 1939); J. Frank Dobie, *The Longhorns* (New York: Bramhall House, 1941), 283.

4. Barry Lopez, "Renegotiating the Contracts," *Parabola* 8 (Spring 1983): 18.

5. Paul Russell Cutright, *Lewis and Clark: Pioneering Naturalists* (Lincoln: University of Nebraska Press, 1969), 142, 424–47. Altogether Cutright lists 122 species and subspecies discovered by the explorers, 65 west of the Continental Divide and 57 east. See also Raymond Darwin Burroughs, *The Natural History of the Lewis and Clark Expedition* (East Lansing: Michigan State University, 1961).

6. *Original Journals of the Lewis and Clark Expedition, 1804–1806*, ed. by Reuben Gold Thwaites (New York: Arno Press, 1904), 1:345, 2:3–84.

7. *Original Journals* 1:147, 155, 350; 2:93–96.

8. Jeremy Bentham, *An Introduction to the Principles of Morals and Legislation*, ed. by J. H. Burns and H. L. A. Hart (1780; London: University of London, The Athlone Press, 1970), 282–83. Bentham's leading disciple today is Peter Singer, author of *Animal Liberation*, 2d ed. (New York: New York Review of Books, 1990).

9. Useful accounts of the humanitarian movement are E. S. Turner, *All Heaven in a Rage* (London: Michael Joseph, 1964); Gerald Carson, *Men, Beasts, and Gods: A History of Cruelty and Kindness to Animals* (New York: Charles Scribner's Sons, 1972); and James Turner, *Reckoning with the Beast: Animals, Pain, and Humanity in the Victorian Mind* (Baltimore: Johns Hopkins University Press, 1980). See also Keith Thomas, *Man and the Natural World: A History of the Modern Sensibility* (New York: Pantheon, 1983), chapter 4; Harriet Ritvo, *The Animal Estate: The English and Other Creatures in the Victorian Age* (Cambridge, Mass.: Harvard University Press, 1987); and James Serpell, *In the Company of Animals: A Study of Human-Animal Relationships* (Oxford: Basil Blackwell, 1986).

10. Josiah Gregg, *The Commerce of the Prairies*, ed. by Milo Milton Quaife (1844; Lincoln: University of Nebraska Press, 1926), 317–20.

11. Richard Irving Dodge, *The Plains of North America and Their Inhabitants*, ed. by Wayne R. Kime (Newark: University of Delaware Press, 1989), 140, 150, 157. William Hornaday calculated that Dodge's big herd might have numbered half a million animals. According to Theodore Roosevelt, "The bulk of the slaughter was done in the dozen years from 1872 to 1883; never before in all history were so many large wild animals of one species slain in so short a time"; *Hunting Trips of a Ranchman* (New York: G. P. Putnam's, 1886), 108.

12. Dodge, *The Plains*, 138–39. The poor colonel arrived too late in the West to see or shoot a live mountain buffalo, always less numerous than their plains counterparts. After puffing up and down the Rockies in 1877, he came home empty-handed. "My figure," he lamented, "is no longer adapted to mountain climbing and the possession of a bison's head of my own killing is one of my blighted hopes"; *ibid.*, 145.

13. Maxine Benson, ed., *From Pittsburgh to the Rocky Mountains: Major Stephen Long's Expedition, 1819–1820* (Golden, Colo.: Fulcrum Press, 1988), 183; John Francis McDermott, ed., *Audubon in the West* (Norman: University of Oklahoma Press, 1965), 115; John C. Frémont, *The Exploring Expedition to the Rocky Mountains* (1845; Washington, D.C.: Smithsonian Institution Press, 1988), 19. See also Major John B. Jeffrey, "Animal Life on the Pacific Coast Some Fifty Years Ago," *Overland Monthly* 51 (June 1908):534–36; and Ellers Koch, "Big Game in Montana from Early Historical Records," *Journal of Wildlife Management* 5 (October 1941):357–70.

14. Ernest Thompson Seton, *Lives of the Hunted* (New York: Charles Scribner's Sons, 1901), 9; Seton, *Wild Animals I Have Known* (New York: Charles Scribner's Sons, 1926), 11–12; Farida A. Wiley, ed., *Ernest Thompson Seton's America* (New York: Devin- Adair, 1954), xxiii. For accounts of his life and thought, see H. Allen Anderson, *The Chief: Ernest Thompson Seton and the Changing West* (College Station: Texas A&M University Press, 1986); John Henry Wadland, *Ernest Thompson Seton: Man and Nature and the Progressive Era, 1880–1915* (New York: Arno Press, 1978); and Lisa Mighetto, *Wild Animals and American Environmental Ethics* (Tucson: University of Arizona Press, 1991), 86–88.

15. Ernest Thompson Seton, *Lives of Game Animals* (Garden City, N.Y.: Doubleday, Doran, 1929), 1, part 1:258–65; 2, part 1:21. Two books carefully document the decline of these major predators in New Mexico and Arizona: David E. Brown, *The Grizzly in the Southwest: Documentary of an Extinction* (Norman: University of Oklahoma Press, 1985); and David E. Brown, ed., *The Wolf in the Southwest: The Making of an Endangered Species* (Tucson: University of Arizona Press, 1983). Mountain lions, along with grizzlies and wolves, had once been common to the Plains but had retreated back into timbered country. The largest cat in the New World, the jaguar, was also a regular presence on the Plains and throughout the Southwest; as late as 1946, a two-hundred-pound jaguar was found in south Texas. See Arthur F. Halloran, "The Extinct and

Vanishing Wildlife of the Great Plains," *Great Plains Journal* 12 (Spring 1973):194–200.

16. Seton, *Lives of Game Animals*, 3, part 1:14, 335–36; 3, part 2:426–27, 534–35, 540; 4, part 1:280; 4, part 2:447–48.

17. Seton, *Lives of Game Animals*, 3, part 2:426, 534–35, 654–55; 3, part 1:14, 335; 4, part 1:280; 4, part 2:447–48. Seton broke his bison total into 40 million living in the plains area, 30 million on the prairies, and 5 million in the forests, figures all based on potential food supply. The best account of this animal's fate is David A. Dary, *The Buffalo Book: The Saga of an American Symbol* (Chicago: Swallow Press, 1974), especially chapter 7. See also Philip Drennon Thomas, "The Near Extinction of the American Bison: A Case Study in Legislative Lethargy," *Western American History in the Seventies*, ed. by Daniel Tyler (Fort Collins, Colo.: Robinson Press, 1973), 21–33.

18. A good survey of this subject, though perhaps dated, is *The Native Population of the Americas in 1942*, ed. by William M. Denevan (Madison: University of Wisconsin, 1976). Dobyns, in *Their Number Became Thinned: Native American Population Dynamics in Eastern North America* (Knoxville: University of Tennessee, 1983), 34–45, argues that 18 million natives lived north of civilized Mesoamerica in the early years of the sixteenth century. Obviously this is a topic on which scholarly opinion varies widely.

19. Frank Gilbert Roe, *The North American Buffalo: A Critical Study of the Species in Its Wild State* (Toronto: University of Toronto Press, 1951), 505. Roe argued that Seton erred in assuming that the potential bison range was crowded to capacity. See also Dan Flores, "Bison Ecology and Bison Diplomacy: The Southern Plains from 1800 to 1850," *Journal of American History* 78 (September 1991):471. Another estimate comes from Tom McHugh, who believes that the carrying capacity of the grasslands has been exaggerated; a single buffalo would need about 25 acres of grass (a mean average of short and tallgrass prairies), giving a continental total of 30 million; *The Time of the Buffalo* (Lincoln: University of Nebraska Press, 1972), 16–17.

20. A. Starker Leopold, Ralph J. Gutierrez, and Michael T. Bronson, *North American Game Birds and Mammals* (New York: Charles Scribner's Sons, 1981), 162, 165.

21. Frederic H. Wagner, "Livestock Grazing and the Livestock Industry," *Wildlife and America*, ed. by Howard P. Brokaw (Washington, D.C.: Council on Environmental Quality, 1978), 133–35; Barry Holstun Lopez, *Of Wolves and Men* (New York: Charles Scribner's Sons, 1978), 180.

22. People sometimes assume that the only environmental threats in the West have come from hunting, or from mining or lumbering, when in fact it was agriculture that was the more devastating and permanent force of change. Ducks such as the mallard and pintail lost more to expanding cereal producers, who drained and plowed their potholes and marshes, and the sandhill crane lost more to farmers diverting the Platte River into their fields, than to hunters. Today the

country has less than half of its original wetlands left—from an estimated pre-Columbian area of 215 million acres in the continental Unites States.

23. Frank B. Linderman, *Plenty-Coups, Chief of the Crows* (1930; Lincoln: University of Nebraska Press, 1957), 73, 252, 311–12.

24. James B. Trefethen, *An American Crusade for Wildlife* (New York: Winchester Press and the Boone and Crockett Club, 1975); Thomas R. Dunlap, *Saving America's Wildlife* (Princeton, N.J.: Princeton University Press, 1988); Lisa Mighetto, *Wild Animals*; John F. Reiger, *American Sportsmen and the Origins of Conservation*, rev. ed. (1975; Norman: University of Oklahoma Press, 1986), especially chapter 1.

25. George Bird Grinnell,"A Plank," *Forest and Stream* (1894), cited in Reiger, *American Sportsmen*, 32. Grinnell was the central figure in the founding of the first Audubon Society (1886), dedicated to the conservation of birds, and of the Boone and Crockett Club (1887), whose mission was to save the larger game animals. Membership in the latter was limited to one hundred men who had killed at least one individual of three of the various kinds of large game. Members came from well-to-do New York families, including the Roosevelts. See John F. Reiger, "A Dedication to the Memory of George Bird Grinnell, 1849–1938," *Arizona and the West* 21 (Spring 1979):1–4; and Albert Kendrick Fisher, "In Memoriam: George Bird Grinnell," *The Auk* 56 (January 1939):1–12.

26. James A. Tober, *Who Owns the Wildlife? The Political Economy of Conservation in Nineteenth-Century America* (Westport, Conn.: Greenwood Press, 1981), 153, 155, 158, 160. In legal tradition the states, not the federal government, owned all wildlife, though after the Lacey Act, the federal government began to take on more responsibility for wildlife protection and restoration, leaving hunting laws and their enforcement to the states.

27. George Bird Grinnell and Charles Sheldon, eds., *Hunting and Conservation: The Book of the Boone and Crockett Club* (New Haven: Yale University Press, 1925), xi, 219–20, 500–501, 510–11.

28. Funds for land acquisition at first came through New Deal relief programs, but the Migratory Bird Stamp Act of 1934 made the selling of duck stamps the main method of purchase, and then in 1937 the Federal Aid in Wildlife Restoration Act (popularly known as Pitt-Robertson) levied an excise tax on sales of firearms and ammunition and distributed the revenues to the states for conservation work. Today there are 450 units in the national wildlife-refuge system, and they cover over 90 million acres of land and water, while states have used their federal funds to acquire over 4 million more acres. See Ira N. Gabrielson, *Wildlife Refuges* (New York: Macmillan, 1943), chapter 1; and Winston Harrington, "Wildlife: Severe Decline and Partial Recovery," *America's Renewable Resources: Historical Trends and Current Challenges*, ed. by Kenneth D. Frederick and Roger A. Sedjo (Washington, D.C.: Resources for the Future, 1991), 217–23. Hornaday's comment comes from Trefethen, 257.

29. For an overview of the period, see Theodore W. Cart, "'New Deal' for Wildlife: A Perspective on Federal Conservation Policy, 1933–40," *Pacific Northwest Quarterly* 63 (July 1972):113–20. Offsetting the real gains were immense losses to wildlife habitat caused by western reclamation projects.

30. Wagner, "Livestock Grazing," 124. According to a federal survey, 84 percent of the public range was in poor or only fair condition; *The Western Range*, Senate Document 199, 74th Congress, 2d Session, Serial Number 10005 (Washington, D.C.: Government Printing Office, 1936), 81–116. John Muir, *The Mountains of California* (1894; Garden City, N.Y.: Natural History Library, 1961), 268.

31. Albert M. Day and Almer P. Nelson, "Wild Life Conservation and Control in Wyoming under the Leadership of the United States Biological Survey (n.p., n.d.). I have discussed the early history of predator control in *Nature's Economy: A History of Ecological Ideas* (New York: Cambridge University Press, 1977), chapter 13. See also Dunlap, *Saving America's Wildlife*, 47–61,

32. William T. Hornaday, *Wild Life Conservation in Theory and Practice* (New Haven: Yale University Press, 1914), 143, 148.

33. Elliott S. Barker, *When the Dogs Bark 'Treed': A Year on the Trail of the Longtails* (Albuquerque: University of New Mexico Press, 1946), x, 9, 135; Barker, *Beatty's Cabin* (Albuquerque: University of New Mexico Press, 1953), 89, 93, 219. For the environmental history of Barker's favorite country, see William deBuys, *Enchantment and Exploitation: The Life and Hard Times of a New Mexico Mountain Range* (Albuquerque: University of New Mexico Press, 1985), especially chapter 10.

34. Aldo Leopold, "The Varmint Question" [1915], *The River of the Mother of God and Other Essays*, ed. by Susan L. Flader and J. Baird Callicott (Madison: University of Wisconsin Press, 1991), 47; Leopold, *Game Management* (1933; Madison: University of Wisconsin Press, 1986), 3. Curt Meine discusses the New Mexico wildlife scene in his biography, *Aldo Leopold: His Life and Work* (Madison: University of Wisconsin Press, 1988), chapters 7–11.

35. Bureau of Biological Survey, "Big-Game Inventory of the United States, 1938," Wildlife Leaflet BS-142 (Washington, D.C.: Government Printing Office, 1939).

36. The quotation is from a book review in the *Journal of Forestry*, 32 (October 1934):775.

37. Aldo Leopold, "Conservation: In Whole or In Part?" *The River of the Mother of God*, 310–19.

38. The first area officially designated as federally protected wilderness was a 500,000-acre area in the Gila National Forest in 1924, and Leopold was the key figure in that designation. Originally, however, the idea seems to have come from Arthur Carhart, a Forest Service employee in Colorado. See Donald N. Baldwin, "Wilderness: Concept and Challenge," *Colorado Magazine* 44 (Summer 1967):224–40. In 1964 Congress passed the National Wilderness Preservation

Act, a step that is fully discussed by Roderick Nash in *Wilderness and the American Mind*, 3d ed. (New Haven: Yale University Press, 1982), chapter 12.

39. Susan L. Flader, *Thinking Like a Mountain: Aldo Leopold and the Evolution of an Ecological Attitude toward Deer, Wolves, and Forests* (Columbia: University of Missouri Press, 1974), 28–35. See also her essay "Scientific Resource Management: An Historical Perspective," *Transactions of the North American Wildlife and Natural Resources Conference* 41 (1976):17–20

40. Leopold, *The River of the Mother of God*, 266–67.

41. Leopold, *The River of the Mother of God*, 210, 317–19; "The Land Ethic," *Sand County Almanac and Sketches Here and There* (1947; New York: Oxford University Press, 1987), 204. For an account of how Leopold stitched together the "Land Ethic" essay from his previous writings, see Meine, *Aldo Leopold*, 501–4.

42. For an example of Leopold's attitude toward the prevailing business, particularly the tourist-industry, mentality, see "A Criticism of the Booster Spirit" [1923], *The River of the Mother of God*, 98–105. On his New Deal–era politics, see Meine, *Aldo Leopold*, 320.

43. That the public has been changing its attitudes toward wild animals faster than the professionals is apparent from the professionals' own writings; see, for example, Durward L. Allen, "Need for a New North American Wildlife Policy," *Transactions of the North American Wildlife and Natural Resources Conference* 37 (1972):45–56; William W. Shaw, "Meanings of Wildlife for Americans: Contemporary Attitudes and Social Trends," *ibid.* 39 (1974):151–55; Jackson J. Jeffrey, "Public Support for Nongame and Endangered Wildlife Management: Which Way Is It Going?" *ibid.* 47 (1982):432–40; Richard D. Taber, "Toward the Progress of Wildlife Conservation in North America," *ibid.* 48 (1983):48–72; and Victor B. Scheffer, "The Future of Wildlife Management," *Wildlife Society Bulletin* 4 (Summer 1976):51–54. For differences between the general public and rural landowners, see Stephen R. Kellert, "Public Attitudes toward Critical Wildlife and Natural Habitat Issues," U.S. Fish and Wildlife Service (Washington, D.C.: Government Printing Office, 1979).

44. A. Starker Leopold, et al., "The National Wildlife Refuge System," *Transactions of the North American Wildlife and Natural Resources Conference* 33 (1968):33. See also the other reports: "Wildlife Management in the National Parks," *ibid.* 28 (1963):28–44; and "Predator and Rodent Control in the United States," *ibid.* 29 (1964):27–49. For a confused, bitter attack on this new philosophy, see Alston Chase, *Playing God in Yellowstone: The Destruction of America's First National Park* (Boston: Atlantic Monthly Press, 1986), especially chapter 4. Chase is eager to interfere and manage, but is vague about what the ends of that interference ought to be: "helping" wildlife or satisfying humans?

45. The literature on the Endangered Species Act is enormous. I have found especially useful the following: Michael J. Bean, *The Evolution of National Wildlife Law* (New York: Praeger, 1983); George C. Coggins, "Conserving

Wildlife Resources: An Overview of the Endangered Species Act of 1973," *North Dakota Law Review* 51 (1975):315–37; Kathryn A. Kohn, ed., *Balancing on the Brink of Extinction: The Endangered Species Act and Lessons for the Future* (Washington, D.C.: Island Press, 1991); and Suzanne Winckler, "Stopgap Measures," *Atlantic Monthly* 269 (January 1992):74–82.

46. See Carolyn Merchant, "Earthcare: Women and the Environmental Movement," *Environment* 23 (June 1981):6–13, 38–40; and *Radical Ecology: The Search for a Livable World* (New York: Routledge, 1992), chapter 8. Also Vera Norwood, *Made from This Earth: American Women and Nature* (Chapel Hill: University of North Carolina Press, 1993), chapters 5 and 7.

47. Wildlife professionals have recently begun to pay attention to the animal-rights movement, though often in tense, defensive ways. See, for instance, the symposium on the subject in *Transactions of the North American Wildlife and Natural Resources Conference* 56 (1991):359–99; Daniel J. Decker and Tommy L. Brown, "How Animal Rightists View the 'Wildlife Management–Hunting System,'" *Wildlife Society Bulletin* 15 (1987):599–602; and James W. Goodrich, "Political Assault on Wildlife Management: Is There a Defense?" *ibid.* 44 (1979):326–36.

Chapter 4

1. Intergovernmental Panel on Climate Change, *Climate Change: The IPCC Scientific Assessment*, ed. by J. T. Houghton, G. J. Jenkins, and J. J. Ephraums (Cambridge: Cambridge University Press, 1990). The changes will be caused by increases in the so-called "greenhouse gases." Carbon dioxide is the most important of those gases; during the preindustrial period, and indeed since the end of the last Ice Age, CO_2 has constituted a steady 280 parts per million by volume of the global atmosphere, but by 1990, after so much fossil-fuel burning, it had risen to 353 ppmv and, at a modest 2 percent growth rate, would reach 1100 ppmv by the end of the next century. The other major contributors to global warming include methane, nitrous oxide, and the chlorofluorocarbons. See also Stephen H. Schneider, "The Greenhouse Effect: Science and Policy," *Science* 243 (10 February 1989):771–81.

2. Intergovernmental Panel, *Climate Change*, pp. xi–xii. Also see Geoffrey Wall, ed., *Symposium on the Impacts of Climatic Change and Variability on the Great Plains*, Department of Geography, University of Waterloo, Occasional Paper No. 12 (Waterloo, Ontario, 1991); and Joel B. Smith and Dennis A. Tirpak, eds., *The Potential Effects of Global Climate Change on the United States* (New York: Hemisphere Publishing Corp., 1990), chapter 7.

3. William W. Kellogg and Robert Schware, *Climate Change and Society: Consequences of Increasing Atmospheric Carbon Dioxide* (Boulder: Westview Press, 1981), 65, 157–61. Areas that seem likely to become wetter than now,

improving their agricultural prospects, include central Mexico, the Sahara and East Africa, Saudia Arabia, India, and western Australia. Thus the agricultural impact of global warming may be far more adverse for the United States than for a large part of the so-called developing world.

4. Thomas R. Karl and Richard R. Heim, Jr., "The Greenhouse Effect in Central North America: If Not Now, When?" in *Symposium on the Impacts of Climatic Change and Variability on the Great Plains*, 19–29.

5. I owe these figures to Marty Bender of the Land Institute, Salina, Kansas. See also David Pimental, ed., *Handbook of Energy Utilization in Agriculture* (Boca Raton, Fla.: CRC Press, 1980). It should be added that only 2 percent of all energy consumed in the United States is consumed on the farm; clearly agriculture is going to be more victim than perpetrator of global warming. On the other hand, the heavily rural plains states are among the most intensive users of energy in the world.

6. Donald Worster, *Dust Bowl: The Southern Plains in the 1930s* (New York: Oxford University Press, 1979), 35.

7. According to Karl W. Butzer, "Dust Bowl conditions would become commonplace on the Great Plains, with an increased incidence of drought in the Midwest." See his "Adaptation to Global Environmental Change," *Professional Geographer* 32 (August 1980): 271.

8. Butzer, "Adaptation," 273.

9. Two agricultural economists calculate that "a 3°C increase in regional temperatures and a small reduction in summer precipitation tends to shift the Corn Belt into droughty soils, hence to reduce the region suited for such production by about 30 percent." With a 2°C rise in temperatures and a 10 percent decrease in precipitation, Great Plains wheat yields fall 8 to 15 percent and 6 to 8 percent, respectively. "The soil resource base of the granary, especially on the Great Plains, may [also] be at risk with a major warming. Wind erosion of soils . . . may intensify under drier and droughtier conditions, leading to increased erosion, intensification of current desertification trends, and in the worst case, to dust bowl conditions. . . . Insect populations may increase as much milder winters and frost-free seasons increase the number of insect generations per summer. Grasshoppers, cutworms, corn borers, and aphids may be important as may viruses vectored by insect populations." As for the prospects of overcoming these conditions through plant breeding, they add, "it has not yet been proven possible to incorporate significantly enhanced heat or drought tolerance into present cultivars without lower average yields. . . . Adaptive capability in this regard has been limited both by technological and income constraints, and given current trends in agricultural income, these appear unlikely to lessen in the future. Traditional plant breeding techniques might be able to adapt present cultivars somewhat at the margin, perhaps to several tenths of a degree Celsius per decade. However, adaptations to more rapid changes, for instance 0.3 to 0.8 C° per decade, seem beyond the power of

these techniques. Revolutionary alterations in the genetic makeup of American crops, one frequently cited potential adaptation, might alter this situation. However, such alterations have yet to be demonstrated. The adaptive capability of the agricultural system, in this case, probably ought to be considered rather limited from the perspective of major alterations in crop physiology until the prospects of genetic engineering have been substantiated." Peter Ciborowski and Dean Abrahamson, "The Granary and the Greenhouse Problem," in *The Future of the North American Granary: Politics, Economics, and Resource Constraints in North American Agriculture*, ed. by C. Ford Runge (Ames: Iowa State University Press, 1986), 70–73.

10. *New York Times*, 7 September 1991.

11. Martyn J. Bowden, "The Great American Desert and the American Frontier, 1800–1882: A Problem in Historical Geosophy," in *Anonymous Americans: Explanations in Nineteenth-Century Social History*, ed. by Tamara Hareven (Englewood Cliffs, N.J.: Prentice-Hall, 1971), 48–79. See also Bowden, "The Great American Desert in the American Mind: The Historiography of a Geographical Notion," in *Geographies of the Mind: Essays in Historical Geosophy*, ed. by David Lowenthal and Martyn J. Bowden (New York: Oxford University Press, 1976), 119–48; and *Images of the Plains: The Role of Human Nature in Settlement*, ed. by Brian W. Blouet and Merlin P. Lawson (Lincoln: University of Nebraska Press, 1975).

12. Wright Morris, *God's Country and My People* (New York: Harper and Row, 1968), n.p. The standard account of this overwrought optimism is Henry Nash Smith, "Rain Follows the Plow: The Notion of Increased Rainfall for the Great Plains, 1844–1880," *Huntington Library Quarterly* 10 (February 1947):169–93. The most influential scientist supporting climate meliorism was Samuel Aughey of the University of Nebraska, who believed that through planting trees, humans could lend "a helping hand to the processes of nature for the development and utilization of the material wealth" of the region; Smith, "Rain Follows the Plow," 184–85. See also Clark C. Spence, *The Rainmakers: American "Pluviculture" to World War II* (Lincoln: University of Nebraska Press, 1980).

13. C. Warren Thornthwaite, "Climate and Settlement in the Great Plains," *Climate and Men: Yearbook of Agriculture*, 1941 (Washington, D.C.: Government Printing Office, 1941), 178.

14. Joseph B. Kincer, "The Climate of the Great Plains as a Factor in Their Utilization," *Annals of the Association of American Geographers* 13 (June 1923):67–80.

15. J. B. Kincer, "Probable Frequency of Serious Nation-Wide Droughts in the United States," *Agricultural Engineering* 13 (June 1932):146. As the dust storms began to blow in 1934, Kincer tried to refute popular notions that humans were responsible for drought. Some people, for instance, blamed the lack of rainfall on excessive drainage of wetlands and ponds, while one crank offered to call the

drought off when people accepted "his philosophic convictions"; Kincer, "Man's Responsibility for Droughts in the Great Plains," *Bulletin of the American Meteorological Society* 16 (May 1935):146–48.

16. Frederick E. Clements, "Drouth Periods and Climatic Cycles," *Ecology* 2 (July 1921):181–88. For a more recent study of the same question, see J. M. Mitchell, C. W. Stockton, and D. M. Meko, "Evidence of a 22-Year Rhythm of Drought in the Western United States Related to the Hale Solar Cycle since the 17th Century," in *Solar-Terrestrial Influences on Weather and Climate*, ed. by B. McCormac and T. A. Seliga (Dordrecht, Holland: D. Reidel, 1979), 125–43. For an overview of the history of weather forecasting, see Alan D. Hecht, "Drought in the Great Plains: History of Societal Response," *Journal of Climate and Applied Meteorology* 22 (January 1983):51–56.

17. An Englishman named Harriot has been credited with discovering in 1610 that there are spots on the sun, and the astronomer Galileo Galilei published a paper on them three years later. See Ivan Ray Tannehill, *Drought: Its Causes and Effects* (Princeton, N.J.: Princeton University Press, 1947), 143–44. See also Hubert H. Lamb, *Weather, Climate and Human Affairs: A Book of Essays and Other Papers* (Routledge: London and New York, 1988), 333, which discusses the important sunspot work of H. C. Willett.

18. See Ellsworth Huntington, *The Climatic Factor as Illustrated in Arid America* (Washington, D.C.: Carnegie Institutions of Washington, 1914), chapter 19. See also his book *Earth and Sun* (New Haven: Yale University Press, 1923).

19. Charles W. Stockton and David M. Meko, "Drought Recurrence in the Great Plains as Reconstructed from Long-Term Tree-Ring Records," *Journal of Climate and Applied Meteorology* 22 (January 1983):17–29.

20. This argument is made in James Gleick, *Chaos: The Making of a New Science* (New York: Viking, 1987), especially 15–20, which discuss the revolutionary work of meteorologist Edward Lorenz.

21. Edward N. Lorenz, "Irregularity: A Fundamental Property of the Atmosphere," *Tellus* 36A (1984):108.

22. This conclusion is admitted by a leading climatologist, F. Kenneth Hare, in "Drought and Desiccation: Twin Hazards of a Variable Climate," *Planning for Drought: Toward a Reduction of Societal Vulnerability*, ed. by Donald A. Wilhite and William E. Easterly, with Deborah A. Wood (Boulder: Westview Press, 1987), 5. Hare writes: "Why does rainfall sometimes fail? Amazingly there is no clear answer. . . . drought is still largely unpredictable, and its causes are obscure" (ibid.). See also Schneider, "The Greenhouse Effect," 775–76, where he admits that the actual warming that has occurred over the past hundred years is less than the present models would have predicted.

23. *The Future of the Great Plains*, House Document 144, 75th Congress, 1st session, 63–64.

24. *Future of the Great Plains*, 76.

25. James Earl Sherow, *Watering the Valley: Development along the High Plains Arkansas River, 1870–1950* (Lawrence: University Press of Kansas, 1990), 79–100; and Anne M. Marvin, "The Fertile Domain: Irrigation as Adaptation in the Garden City, Kansas Area, 1880–1910" (Ph.D. dissertation, University of Kansas, 1985).

26. Edwin D. Gutentag et al., *Geohydrology of the High Plains Aquifer*, U.S. Geological Survey Professional Paper 1400-B (Washington, D.C.: Government Printing Office, 1984).

27. Cited in Donald E. Green, *Land of the Underground Rain: Irrigation on the Texas High Plains, 1919–1970* (Austin: University of Texas Press, 1973), 230.

28. Jonathan Taylor, Mary W. Downton, and Thomas R. Stewart, "Adapting to Environmental Change: Perceptions and Farming Practices in the Ogallala Aquifer Region," in *Arid Lands Today and Tomorrow*, ed. by Emily E. Whitehead et al. (Boulder: Westview Press, 1988), 666. By the 1970s cattle feedlots in the Ogallala Aquifer area supplied 40 percent of the total production of grain-fed beef in the United States. See John Walsh, "What to Do When the Well Runs Dry," *Science* 210 (14 November 1980):754–56.

29. John Opie, *Ogallala: Water for a Dry Land* (Lincoln: University of Nebraska Press, 1993), chapter 5. The ineffectiveness of the new regulatory agencies may be suggested by the experience of the Nebraska Resources Districts, set up in 1972; despite three consecutive dry years, no NRD took concrete steps to impose groundwater controls until 1977. During that five-year interim, they pursued a technological rather than political solution to the depletion problem. See Robert D. Miewald, "Social and Political Impacts of Drought," in *North American Droughts*, ed. by Norman J. Rosenberg (Boulder: Westview Press, 1978), 95. See also Peter J. Korsching and Peter J. Nowak, "Farmer Acceptance of Alternative Conservation Policies," *Agriculture and Environment* 7 (1982):1–14, which emphasizes the differences among farmers in openness to conservation. However, it is also clear from their data that economic incentives are far more popular among farmers (64 percent of their sample found them acceptable) than legal regulations (59 percent said they were unacceptable).

30. High Plains Associates, *Six-State High Plains–Ogallala Aquifer Regional Resources Study: Summary* (Austin, Texas: Camp Dreser and McKee, 1982); High Plains Study Council, *A Summary of Results of the Ogallala Aquifer Regional Study, with Recommendations to the Secretary of Commerce and Congress* (1982); U.S. Army Corps of Engineers, *Six-State High Plains Ogallala Aquifer Regional Resources Study: Summary Report* (Albuquerque, N. M.: U.S. Army Corps of Engineers, Southwestern Division, 1982).

31. Michael H. Glantz and Jesse H. Ausubel, "The Ogallala Aquifer and Carbon Dioxide: Comparison and Convergence," *Environmental Conservation* 11 (Summer 1984):123–31.

32. A task force on responses to drought, headed by Harold E. Dregne,

concluded that irrigation technology may have increased vulnerability in some cases. They point in particular to center-pivot sprinkler systems, which have permitted the breaking of soils too sandy for irrigation and highly susceptible to wind erosion, systems that have required the removal of shelterbelts planted in the 1930s, because they interfere with the circular sweep of the sprinkler devices. They also have created a false sense of security—a belief that agriculture has achieved freedom from the vicissitudes of climate. Consequently, the task force concluded, "a protracted and widespread drought in western North America is certain to have a far greater impact now than would have been the case twenty years ago." See Norman J. Rosenberg, ed., *Drought in the Great Plains: Research on Impact and Strategies* (Littleton, Colo.: Water Resources Publications, 1979), 20–21.

33. Marc Reisner, *Cadillac Desert: The American West and Its Disappearing Water* (New York: Viking, 1986), 460–67; Donald Worster, *Rivers of Empire: Water, Aridity, and the Growth of the American West* (New York: Pantheon, 1985), 264–65

34. Opie, *Ogallala*, chapter 7. See also Morton W. Bittinger and Elizabeth B. Green, *You Never Miss the Water Till . . . : The Ogallala Story* (Littleton, Colo.: Water Resources Publications, 1980), 90ff.

35. One recent study found considerable disillusionment with irrigation technology among Great Plains farmers. Thirty percent of those questioned agreed that "irrigation, in this country, is a short-term blessing but a long-term curse." The authors of the study concluded that irrigation "is certainly not perceived to be a universal panacea. It involves significantly greater expense, more work, and more time commitment. With rising costs, especially for energy, several farmers described irrigation as 'just chasing dollars," where every dollar increase in output requires at least another dollar input." Taylor, Downton, and Stewart, "Adapting to Environmental Change," 681–82.

36. Wes Jackson, *New Roots for Agriculture* (Lincoln: University of Nebraska Press, 1980), chapter 8. See also Judith D. Soulé and Jon K. Piper, *Farming in Nature's Image: An Ecological Approach to Agriculture* (Covelo, Cal.: Island Press, 1992).

37. Federal crop insurance was begun in 1938 and has continued to the present, with drought as a major cause of claims filed. The insurance allows farmers to recover only their production costs, not the full extent of their losses. This kind of insurance is one that private companies, because of the high risks involved, have been unwilling to offer.

38. The percentage of farm income that comes from government payments has never exceeded 20 percent across the "grassland" states as a whole, including Iowa, Illinois, and Missouri, writes John R. Borchert, in "The Dust Bowl in the 1970s," *Annals of the Association of American Geographers* 61 (March 1971):14. In the mid-thirties government payments came close to 20 percent; they fell to a mere 1–2 percent in the fifties drought, then rose to about 10 percent in 1968.

However, Borchert's figures do not reveal the true picture on the western Plains, the Dust Bowl area proper. There government payments constitute a much higher proportion of farm income, and particularly so in droughty years, when it may exceed 50 percent in some counties.

39. Scott McCartney and Fred Bayles, "Drought Relief Stretches Far Beyond the Need," *Lawrence [Kansas] Journal-World*, Sunday, 17 December 1989, 8D. A useful review of state and federal assistance is given by Donald A. Wilhite, "Government Response to Drought in the United States: With Particular Reference to the Great Plains," *Journal of Climate and Applied Meteorology* 22 (January 1988):40–50.

40. I am summarizing here an argument that has been made by such scholars as Robert Kates, Martyn Bowden, Richard Warrick, and William Riebsame, all associated with the Climate and Research Group at the Center for Technology, Environment, and Development at Clark University. See, for example, Warrick's "Drought in the Great Plains: A Case Study of Research on Climate and Society in the USA," *Climatic Constraints and Human Activities*, ed. by Jesse Ausubel and Asit K. Biswas (Oxford: Pergamon Press, 1980), 93–123. The scholars mentioned above refer to this argument as the "lessening hypothesis" and have accumulated some valuable data to support it; like most hypotheses in historical research, however, it may describe the patterns of the past better than it predicts the future. See also William E. Riebsame, "Managing Drought Impacts on Agriculture: The Great Plains Experience," in *Beyond the Urban Fringe: Land Use Issues of Nonmetropolitan America*, ed. by Rutherford H. Platt and George Macinko (Minneapolis: University of Minnesota Press, 1983), 257–70; and Alan D. Hecht, "Drought in the Great Plains: History of Societal Response," *Journal of Climate and Applied Meteorology* 22 (January 1983):51–56.

41. Lydia Dotto, *Thinking the Unthinkable* (Calgary, Alberta: Wilfrid Laurier University Press/The Calgary Institute for the Humanities, 1987), 37–38.

42. From 1978 to 1983, nearly 600,000 acres of fragile grassland (class IVe, VI, and VII land) in eastern Colorado went under the plow, and over 4.5 million acres in the northern and central Plains. The most important reason for that plowup was, according to a Colorado State University resource economist, "simple economic profit maximization": i.e., raising a wheat crop brought more money than grazing cattle. Paul C. Huszar, "Nature and Causes of the Plowout Problem in Colorado," in Whitehead, *Arid Lands Today*, 663.

43. Earle J. Bedenbaugh, "History of Cropland Set Aside Programs in the Great Plains," in *Impact of the Conservation Reserve Program in the Great Plains*, ed. by John E. Mitchell, USDA, Forest Service, Rocky Mountain Forest and Range Experiment Station, General Technical Report RM-18 (Washington, D.C.: Government Printing Office, 1988), 14. Other papers in this symposium deal with the impact of the CRP on vegetation, wildlife, and human communities.

44. Deborah Epstein Popper and Frank J. Popper, "The Great Plains: From Dust to Dust," *Planning* 53 (December 1987):12–18. More recently they have

called the Buffalo Commons idea only a metaphor for "agricultural pullback," not an actual land-use plan, and allow that private landowners may achieve it as well as any government. I am indebted to them for furnishing me a copy of their unpublished essay, "The Future of the Great Plains" (1992). For a lively account of their reception on the Plains, see Anne Matthews, *Where the Buffalo Roam* (New York: Grove Weidenfeld, 1992).

Index

"A Biotic View of the Land," 84
A Sand County Almanac, 87
acequias, 39
acreages: idled by government rental, 116; in public domain, 27–28, 116, 117, as forest reserve, 20 n 16, as wildlife refuge, 77; irrigated, 32, by deep wells, 105, 106; total western, 14, with available water, 14
adaptation to climate, 94–96; accepting, understanding and predicting climate and, 96–102; control by technology and, 102–109; ecological restoration and, 109–120
Advisory Committee on Wildlife Management, 88
Africa, 48–49
Agricultural Adjustment Administration, 111
Agricultural Stabilization and Conservation Service, 116
agriculture: acreage increases, 115, and overextension, 113, and pushing development, 109–113; agriculture as a cultural construction, 10; crop alternatives, 107; dryland farming, 106; energy required for, 93; government cash for, 110–113; irrigation for, 32, 34–38, 105–106; market hunting and, 74;

native plants in, 109; perennial polyculture, 109; philosophy for, 116; public interest in, 115; rainfall required for, 10; resettlement for, 49, 50; shifting of crop belts, 93–94; technology for, 103–109, and expansion/contraction systems, 100, and no-tillage, 103; water use impact and devastation, 33, 50; water use as secondary for, 40; wild animal control and, 79; wildlife production and, 76. *See also* farming; irrigation; soil
Akosombo Dam, 48, 49
Alaska, 77
alliance for water development, 41, 43, 45–46, 52, 53
Altithermal Period, 92
American Fur Trade of the Far West, The, 57
animal rights, 63, 90
animals: attitude toward, 55–60, 76, 80, 82–85; domestic, 58, 78; laws protecting wildlife, 68; migration of, 118; migratory bird protection, 75; populations of, 66–69; predator control, 70, 78–81, 85, and a report on, 88; propagating wildlife, 75–76; rodents, 78, 79; significant species list, 88–89; species listed by explorers, 61; virtue in ani-